P9-CPV-103

LITTLE HOUSE
Laura Ingalls Wilder

THE WORLD OF LITTLE HOUSE

Carolyn Strom Collins

Christina Wyss Eriksson

ILLUSTRATIONS BY

Deborah Maze

AND Garth Williams

PORTER COUNTY PUBLIC LIBRARY SYSTEM

HarperCollinsPublishers

For Andy and Mark,
with love
—C.S.C. and C.W.E.

To John, Jenny, and Chris
—D.M.

Art on pages i, 12, 24, 38, 50, 62, 74, 86, 98, 110, 144–146, and 148 by Garth Williams.
Art on page 122 by Dan Andreasen.
Photographs are used by permission of the Laura Ingalls Wilder Home Association, Mansfield, Missouri.

HarperCollins®, ☖®, and Little House® are trademarks of HarperCollins Publishers Inc.

The World of Little House
Text copyright © 1996 by Carolyn Collins and Christina Eriksson
Illustrations copyright © 1996 by Deborah Maze
Manufactured in China. For information address HarperCollins Children's Books,
a division of HarperCollins Publishers, 10 East 53rd Street, New York, NY 10022.

Library of Congress Cataloging-in-Publication Data
Collins, Carolyn Strom.
  The world of little house / Carolyn Strom Collins, Christina Wyss Eriksson ; illustrations by Deborah Maze and Garth Williams.
    p.   cm.
  Includes bibliographical references (p.   ).
  Summary: A compendium of biographical and historical anecdotes, recipes, activities, and crafts from the life of Laura
Ingalls Wilder and her nine Little House books.
  ISBN 0-06-024422-4. — ISBN 0-06-024423-2 (lib. bdg.)
  1. Wilder, Laura Ingalls, 1867–1957—Juvenile literature.   2. Authors, American—20th century—Biography—Juvenile
literature.   3. Frontier and pioneer life—West (U.S.)—Juvenile literature.   4. Creative activities and seat work—Juvenile
literature.   5. Cookery, American—Juvenile literature.   6. Handicraft—Juvenile literature.
  [1. Wilder, Laura Ingalls, 1867–1957.   2. Authors, American.   3. Frontier and pioneer life—West (U.S.)
4. Cookery, American.   5. Handicraft.]   I. Eriksson, Christina Wyss.   II. Maze, Deborah, ill.   III. Title.
PS3545.I342Z62   1996   94-46569
813.52—dc20   CIP
[B]   AC

Typography by Alicia Mikles
5   6   7   8   9   10
❖

ACKNOWLEDGMENTS

We gratefully acknowledge the help and encouragement of the many people who were willing to share their knowledge, expertise, and influence to ensure that this book reflects Laura's life and times accurately:

In Pepin, Wisconsin—Lorraine Lindell, Catherine Latané, and Martha Kuhlman of the Laura Ingalls Wilder Memorial Society;

In Independence, Kansas—Brigadier General and Mrs. William Kurtis, owners of the Little House on the Prairie; Jeanne Burton, Register of Deeds; and Rick Kemp, Highway Department;

In Malone, New York—Edward Tattershall and Larry House of the Almanzo and Laura Ingalls Wilder Association;

In Walnut Grove, Minnesota—Shirley Knakmuhs of the Laura Ingalls Wilder Museum;

In De Smet, South Dakota—Vivian Glover of the Laura Ingalls Wilder Memorial Society; Sharon Peterson and Carol Peterson of the Hazel L. Meyer Memorial Library; Lavonne Williams, Register of Deeds; Barbara Geyer, De Smet Depot Museum; and Helen and Leonard Penney, owners of the Ingalls Homestead;

In Mansfield, Missouri—Jean Coday, President, Laura Ingalls Wilder–Rose Wilder Lane Home Association; Elva Bogart and her staff of docents and JoAnn Gray in the administration office at Rocky Ridge;

Our thanks, also, to the University of Missouri Library, Columbia, Missouri; Detroit Public Library, Detroit, Michigan; Marguerite Raybould, Laura Ingalls Wilder Room of the Pomona, California, Public Library; Caroline Collins, Mary Beth Cavert, T. P. O'Leary, and Kathleen Baxter in the Twin Cities; Maria Charlesworth and Ellen Carpenter in Stockholm, Wisconsin; John C. Luecke, author, *The Chicago and Northwestern in Minnesota*; Frank Moertl, Wisconsin Postal History Society, Hartland, Wisconsin; Winona Historical Society, Winona, Minnesota; University of Minnesota Libraries; Minnesota Historical Society; Tracy Railroad Museum, Tracy, Minnesota; Brookings County Historical Society, Brookings, South Dakota; Wright County Historical Society, Wright County, Missouri; Lauri Smalley and Brenda Day, Wright County assessor's office; Lisa Carter and Jaye Wolf in Tempe, Arizona; the writings of William T. Anderson, Donald Zochert, Roger Lea MacBride, and many others.

We very much appreciate the collaboration and guidance of our editors at HarperCollins—Kate Morgan Jackson, Nancy Siscoe, Alix Reid, and Mary-Alice Moore. We especially thank our literary agent, Jeanne Hanson, for her sensible advice on so many occasions. To Deborah Maze goes our complete admiration for her beautiful illustrations of Laura's world.

Finally, to our husbands, Andy and Mark, and to our children, Caroline and Drew, Aaron and Sarah Jane, our thanks for encouraging us to pursue this project even though it meant many days away from our own "little houses."

—C.S.C. and C.W.E.

Contents

Laura Ingalls Wilder, around 1906

Introduction

THE WORLD OF LAURA INGALLS WILDER has been a special place for millions of readers ever since Laura began writing the Little House books in the 1930's. Like many lifetime Little House readers, both of us had read the Little House books as children and then reread them to our own children when we grew up. The more often we read them, the more we loved them and the more we wanted to learn about Laura and her family's life on the frontier. We wondered, for example, what the insides of the little houses might have looked like, what Laura's life was like after she married Almanzo, and how to make and do some of the things Laura described in her books. *The World of Little House* was written for the many, many readers who have asked the very same kinds of questions. It brings together in a single volume all sorts of information about Laura and the Little House books, about the houses, the towns, and the land she describes, and about pioneer life in America.

The first part of *The World of Little House* tells of Laura's many moves and many homes, from her first days in a log cabin in the Big Woods of Wisconsin to her final home in a farmhouse in Mansfield, Missouri. Laura's real life is sometimes different from the life she described in her books, and this chapter talks about some of those differences. It discusses what Laura's adult life was like and how she came to write the Little House books. Also in this chapter are family trees showing four generations of Laura's family and a map of the United States showing all the many places Laura lived.

Each of the following nine chapters revolves around one of the nine Little House books. In these chapters there are floor plans that show the inside of each of Laura's little houses. A few of the original houses still exist—the Surveyors' House in De Smet, Almanzo's *Farmer Boy* home, and the Rocky Ridge farmhouse in Mansfield—and the illustrations in this book are based on these houses. For the rest, Laura's own descriptions in her books and other writings, as well as various historical references, were consulted. Because most of

Laura's houses do not exist anymore, we have had to draw frequently on information about houses typical in Laura's day and from time to time on Garth Williams' well-researched art. There are also drawings in these chapters that show what the outsides of the houses Laura lived in looked like, and what the land was like around those houses.

In her books Laura described some of the happy times she and her family shared as they cooked or baked, or made gifts for each other. In these nine chapters you will find instructions or recipes for some of the things Laura and her family made, such as the clove apple Aunt Eliza gave Ma in *Little House in the Big Woods*, or the shelf paper Laura helped Ma make in *On the Banks of Plum Creek*. In each of these chapters, too, is a section that tells more about a memorable aspect of pioneer life that Laura described in her books. For example, there is a description of general stores in the chapter about *Little House in the Big Woods* and of prairie schools in the chapter about *These Happy Golden Years*.

Included in *The World of Little House* is a chapter about the years Laura spent at Rocky Ridge Farm with her husband, Almanzo, and their daughter, Rose. Laura did not write a book about these years, but it was at Rocky Ridge Farm that Laura raised her own family and it was there that she wrote the Little House books. Also included is a time line that shows the significant events in Laura's life in relation to some significant events that were happening in the United States at the same time.

Compiling all the information in this book required a great deal of research. We reread all the Little House books, and we studied the many books and articles that have been written about Laura and her family and the places in which they lived. There is a bibliography at the end of *The World of Little House* that lists the names of many of these books. We studied Laura's original manuscripts, which were handwritten on paper tablets. We visited all the Little House sites and museums to see for ourselves where Laura and Almanzo lived as children and as adults. We have included a list of all these sites and museums in Chapter 13, along with their addresses and telephone numbers. We consulted libraries, archives, and museum collections to read all of Laura's published and unpublished letters, articles, and diaries, and we consulted books, articles, and experts in many fields for more information about American frontier life. We learned about prairie schools and entertainment, community life, cooking and cleaning methods, handiwork, medical treatments, and other aspects of pioneer life that Laura touched on in her books.

Laura wrote so beautifully of her and her family's experiences on the American frontier—the Wisconsin woods, the Kansas prairie, the Minnesota and Dakota plains. The Ingalls family and the Wilder family were at the forefront of the great crowd of Americans who pressed westward, shaping a continent to fit their dreams of self-reliance and prosperity. We hope that *The World of Little House* will make it possible for those readers who love Laura and her books to learn more about her days on the frontier—days that have now passed, but will never be forgotten.

Laura, around 1918

Laura Ingalls Wilder

We know Laura Ingalls Wilder best through her nine Little House books, which tell the story of her life as a pioneer girl. Much later in life, Laura wrote about these little houses and her experiences in them. But Laura did not write about every place she lived in. There are some things that happened in Laura's real life that are not in her books.

Laura was born in the Big Woods on February 7, 1867. Her Pa's name was Charles Ingalls. He had grown up in New York State and then moved to Wisconsin with his family. Laura's Ma, Caroline Quiner, was one of the first babies born to settlers in the Milwaukee, Wisconsin, area, in a little town called Brookfield. She met Charles when his family bought a farm near her family's farm. They married and in 1863 Pa and Ma decided to move to the Big Woods. Their first daughter, Mary, was born there in 1865, and Laura was born two years later.

When Laura was still a baby, Pa and Ma decided to leave the Big Woods. They moved to a farm near Keytesville, Missouri, and lived there about a year. Then they moved to land on the prairie thirteen miles south of Independence, Kansas. Carrie was born while they lived in Kansas.

After two years in their little house on the prairie, the Ingallses discovered that they could not claim the land they lived on because it belonged to the Osage Indians. So they went back to the Big Woods and lived in the very same house they had left three years earlier!

Charles and Caroline Ingalls, around 1860

This time the Ingallses stayed in the Big Woods for three years. These were the years that Laura wrote about in her first book, *Little House in the Big Woods*. Laura based her second book, *Little House on the Prairie*, on the two years she and her family had lived on the Kansas prairie. Although in real life Laura was only a toddler during her prairie days, in the book she writes that she is five years old, so that this book would smoothly follow *Little House in the Big Woods*.

In the winter of 1874, Ma and Pa decided once again to move. This time they would move west, though, instead of south. They sold their Big Woods farm and crossed the frozen river into Minnesota. They lived for a few months in an abandoned cabin near the river to wait for warmer weather. When spring came, they continued their journey and finally found a beautiful farm near Walnut Grove in southwestern Minnesota. It was on the banks of Plum Creek, just a few miles from town. Laura was now seven years old.

The next two years were hard ones for the Ingallses, and Laura describes some of their hardships in *On the Banks of Plum Creek*. Swarms of grasshoppers devoured all the crops in the area, and Ma and Pa could not pay off all their debts. Finally, they decided they could no longer keep the farm on Plum Creek. Some friends were leaving for Iowa to run a hotel and asked the Ingallses to help them. Pa sold the farm, and they packed the wagon again. Mary, Laura, and Carrie now had a baby brother, Charles Frederic, whom they called Freddie. On the way to

Iowa, Freddie got very sick and died. The trip to Iowa was a sad one.

Laura did not write a book about her year in Burr Oak, Iowa, perhaps because she did not like living in a town at that time. She and her family lived in three places in Burr Oak—first in the hotel, then in rooms over a grocery store, and finally in a little brick house on the edge of town. Laura helped Ma and Pa in the hotel, went to school, took singing lessons, and helped take care of her new baby sister, Grace, who was born in Burr Oak in May 1877.

Ma and Pa were not very happy in Burr Oak, either, and the family returned to Walnut Grove. They stayed with friends in town for the winter. In the spring, Pa built a house on a lot in town. He worked at a store and started a butcher shop of his own. Laura was ten years old now, and she began to earn a little money for the family. She helped in the dining room of the hotel in Walnut Grove. She also baby-sat and ran errands.

Mary and Laura went to the school in Walnut Grove, and Laura went to *two* Sunday Schools, one in the morning at the Congregational Church and one in the afternoon at the Methodist Church. Every Sunday Laura had to memorize a Bible verse. She had such a good memory that she won a contest at the Methodist Sunday School. She recited fifty-two Bible verses and fifty-two "Central Truths" perfectly! Laura won a beautiful new Bible with a special clasp on it. She kept that Bible all her life.

Life in Walnut Grove was busy but difficult. Mary became very ill and then went blind. The family fell into debt again. So Pa decided

Carrie, Mary, and Laura, around 1880

to work for the newly organized Dakota Central Railroad Company as a book-keeper. The family moved once more and claimed land near what would soon become the little town of De Smet in Dakota Territory. Laura wrote about this journey in *By the Shores of Silver Lake*.

It was in De Smet that the Ingalls family finally settled down. Laura was now twelve and had lived in at least twelve little houses. She lived in De Smet for thirteen years, from 1879 to 1890, and once again from 1892 to 1894, and Ma and Pa never moved again. It was in De Smet that Laura's family would endure the endless blizzards of 1880–81, which Laura described in *The Long Winter*. Laura would grow into a young lady in De Smet, going to school, teaching, and working as a seamstress. She would help add to the fund to send Mary to the School for the Blind in Iowa, and she would help Ma and Pa convert their little piece of prairie into the family farm. She would also meet and marry Almanzo Wilder, whose boyhood she wrote about in *Farmer Boy*. In *Little Town on the Prairie* and *These Happy Golden Years*, Laura described the happy and exciting years she lived in De Smet.

Laura and Almanzo were married in 1885 and moved into their own little house several miles from Laura's parents. They lived on their tree claim and worked on their farm. In December 1886, their daughter, Rose, was born.

Laura and Almanzo, around 1885

Life was not easy for the young couple. By the spring of 1890, Laura and Almanzo had endured too many hardships to continue farming in South Dakota. Their house had burned down in 1889, and even worse, their second child, a boy, had died before he was a month old. Drought had ruined their crops year after year, and Almanzo's health had suffered as a result of diphtheria. Laura described these sad months in *The First Four Years*. It was time for a change.

First, Laura, Almanzo, and Rose went east to

Schofield. · Spring Valley, Minn.

Rose at age three

Spring Valley, Minnesota, to live with Almanzo's family. About a year later they moved south to Florida in hopes that the warmer climate would help Almanzo. Laura did not like Florida, though, and the family returned to De Smet within a year. They bought a house in town to live in while saving enough money to buy a farm in Missouri.

In August of 1894, Laura, Almanzo, and Rose left De Smet for good and settled in Mansfield, Missouri, on a piece of land they named Rocky Ridge. They cleared the land, planted hundreds of apple trees, and eventually made Rocky Ridge into a family farm. Laura developed quite a reputation for raising hens. Over a period of about twenty years, Laura and Almanzo built a large white farmhouse to replace the log cabin in which they had started out. Laura and Almanzo never moved again.

When Laura was in her fifties, she began to write down her memories of her pioneer childhood, with the encouragement of her daughter. She realized that life had changed radically since her childhood years of covered wagons and log cabins. The open prairies out west had quickly developed into ranches and farms. Cars and trains had replaced the horse and wagon. Indoor plumbing and electricity were becoming commonplace. Laura wanted to preserve her father's stories of life on the frontier and her own stories of helping to settle the Great Plains.

Laura called her first manuscript *Pioneer*

Rose Wilder Lane

Girl. Based on her own life, it covered the time when she was very little until her marriage with Almanzo. Although this manuscript was never accepted for publication, Laura revised and rewrote it over the years. Finally, in 1931, when Laura was 64 years old, *Little House in the Big Woods* was accepted by the children's department at the Harper and Brothers publishing house in New York. The book was published during the Great Depression, at a time when publishers accepted very few books by unknown authors. But the editor wrote of Laura's book, "Here was a book no Depression could stop."

A well-known artist of that era, Helen Moore Sewell, was chosen to illustrate *Little House in the Big Woods*, and the seven other soon-to-follow Little House books. Helen Sewell had begun her career designing greeting cards, but by the time she began illustrating the Little House series, she had illustrated nine other children's books. In fact, because she was in such great demand as an illustrator, another artist, Mildred Boyle, collaborated with her on the Little House books.

In April of 1932, *Little House in the Big Woods* was published. It was an immediate success and Laura was asked to write more books about her life on the frontier. Her next book, *Farmer Boy,* was published in 1933. The other books quickly followed— *Little House on the Prairie* in 1935, *On the Banks of Plum Creek* in 1937, *By the Shores of Silver Lake* in 1939, *The Long Winter* in 1940, *Little Town on the Prairie* in 1941, and *These Happy Golden Years* in 1943. All the books were very popular and won many awards. The last

Laura and Almanzo in the early 1940's

five were named Newbery Honor award books.

After the entire series of the Little House books had been published, Harper and Brothers decided to reissue the books with new illustrations. They chose Garth Williams as the new illustrator, who had already become well known as the illustrator of *Stuart Little* and *Charlotte's Web*, both by E. B. White. Garth Williams spent several years carefully researching Laura's books to ensure that his illustrations were as historically accurate as possible. He traveled to each of the Little House sites and even visited Laura and Almanzo at Rocky Ridge Farm. The newly illustrated editions were published in 1953 to great acclaim, and have continued to please readers all over the world ever since.

Laura died on February 10, 1957, three days after her ninetieth birthday and eight years after Almanzo died. Children and adults alike were saddened by the news of her death. But interest in the Little House books continued to grow, and has grown only greater with each passing year. After Laura died, two more of her manuscripts were discovered among her papers. These were published to add to the Little House series. *On the Way Home*, Laura's diary of her trip with Almanzo and Rose from De Smet to Mansfield, was published in 1962. In 1971, *The First Four Years*, which tells of the early years of Laura and Almanzo's marriage, was published. And in 1974, *West From Home*, a collection of Laura's letters, which Laura sent to Almanzo when she was visiting Rose in San Francisco, was published. There was even a long-running television series based on the Little House books, called *Little House on the Prairie*. It began in 1974, and the reruns are still popular today.

Since their first publication many years ago, the Little House books have been read by millions of readers all over the world. The books have been translated into dozens of languages, including Japanese, Swahili, Dutch, and Arabic. Many books and articles have been written about the Little House series and about their beloved author. Many of the places Laura lived in as a child and as an adult have been turned into museums. Each year thousands of people visit these sites to see the places that Laura made so memorable in her Little House books and to get a little bit closer to Laura herself.

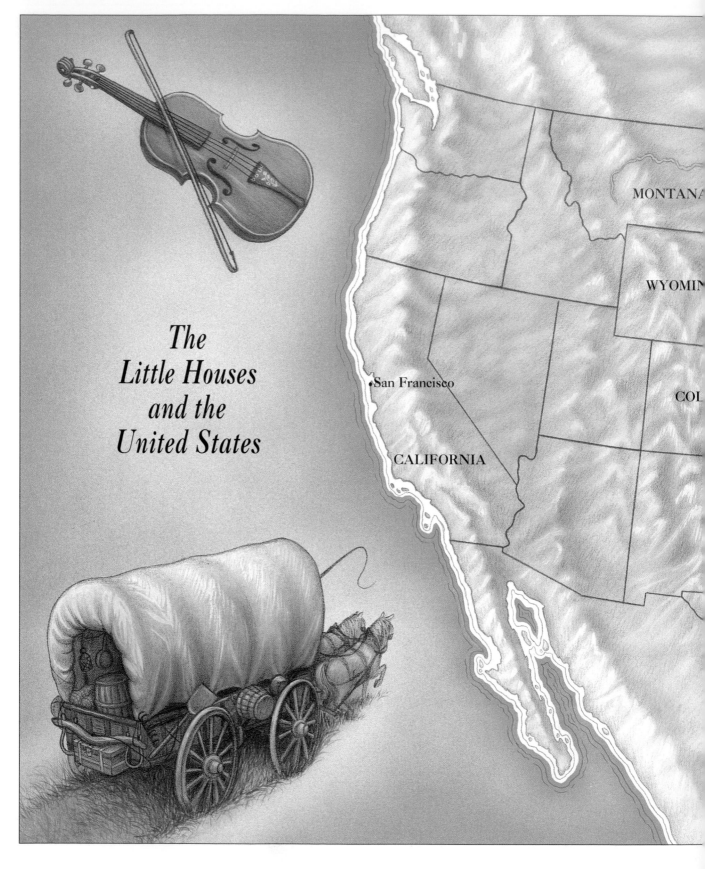

The
Little Houses
and the
United States

San Francisco

CALIFORNIA

MONTANA

WYOMIN

CO

Ingalls Family Tree

Lansford Whiting Ingalls (1812–1896)

Laura Colby (1810–1883)

m.1832

| Peter Riley (1833–1900) | Charles Phillip (1836–1902) | Lydia Louisa (1838–1915) | Polly Melona (1840–1886) | Lansford James (1842–1928) | Laura Ladocia (1845–1918) | Hiram Lemuel (b.1848–d.?) | George Whiting (1851–1901) | Ruby Celestial (1855–1881) | Lansford Clough (1857–d.?) |

m.1860

| Mary Amelia (1865–1928) | Laura Elizabeth (1867–1957) | Caroline Celestia (1870–1946) | Charles Frederic (1875–1876) | Grace Pearl (1877–1941) |

m.1885

Gillette Lane (1887–1950)

Rose (1886–1968)

Baby son (b./d. 1889)

m.1909
div.1918
Baby son (b./d.1910)

—10—

Quiner Family Tree

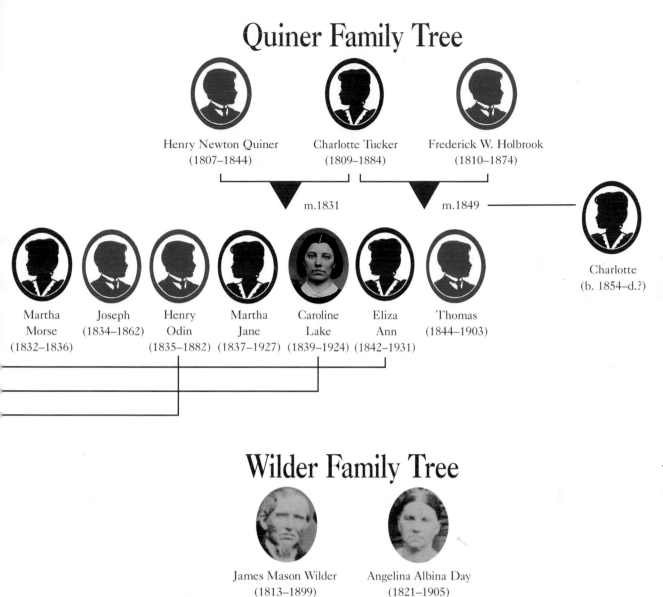

Henry Newton Quiner
(1807–1844)

Charlotte Tucker
(1809–1884)

Frederick W. Holbrook
(1810–1874)

m.1831

m.1849

Charlotte
(b. 1854–d.?)

Martha
Morse
(1832–1836)

Joseph
(1834–1862)

Henry
Odin
(1835–1882)

Martha
Jane
(1837–1927)

Caroline
Lake
(1839–1924)

Eliza
Ann
(1842–1931)

Thomas
(1844–1903)

Wilder Family Tree

James Mason Wilder
(1813–1899)

Angelina Albina Day
(1821–1905)

m.1843

Laura
Ann
(1844–1899)

Royal
Gould
(1847–1925)

Eliza
Jane
(1850–1930)

Alice
(1853–1892)

Almanzo
James
(1857–1949)

Perley
(1869–1934)

Little House in the Big Woods

Once upon a time . . . a little girl lived in the Big Woods
of Wisconsin, in a little gray house made of logs.

LITTLE HOUSE IN THE BIG WOODS introduces readers to Laura Ingalls and her loving family—her Ma and Pa, her big sister, Mary, and her baby sister, Carrie. The book describes a year of Laura's life in the Big Woods of Wisconsin, beginning in the winter of 1871 when Laura was four years old.

Laura's days in the Big Woods were filled with things to do. Every day, she and Mary helped Ma wash the dishes and make the beds. Then, depending on which day of the week it was, they helped Ma with different chores. They helped wash, iron, and mend clothes, churn butter, and bake bread. One day a week they helped clean the cabin. In the winter, Ma taught Mary and Laura how to sew and knit. In the summer, Ma showed them how to grow and preserve fruits and vegetables to store for winter. Laura and Mary also helped Ma make cheese and soap to last through the year.

After their work was done, Mary and Laura could play with their dolls or play games that Ma taught them. When the windows were frosted with ice, they made "thimble pictures" on the windows. In the summer, they played in the yard under the two big oak trees.

Pa spent most of the winter days hunting. He hiked all over the Big Woods with his gun to look for deer or rabbits or even a bear to bring home for dinner.

He set out traps for animals, too, because he needed furs to trade for supplies at the store seven miles away in Pepin.

One day, Pa took the whole family to town with him. Laura and Mary had never been to town before, so the trip was a very special occasion for them. They went to the general store in Pepin to buy cloth and sugar and other goods. Then they had a picnic on the shore of Lake Pepin.

The little house in the Big Woods

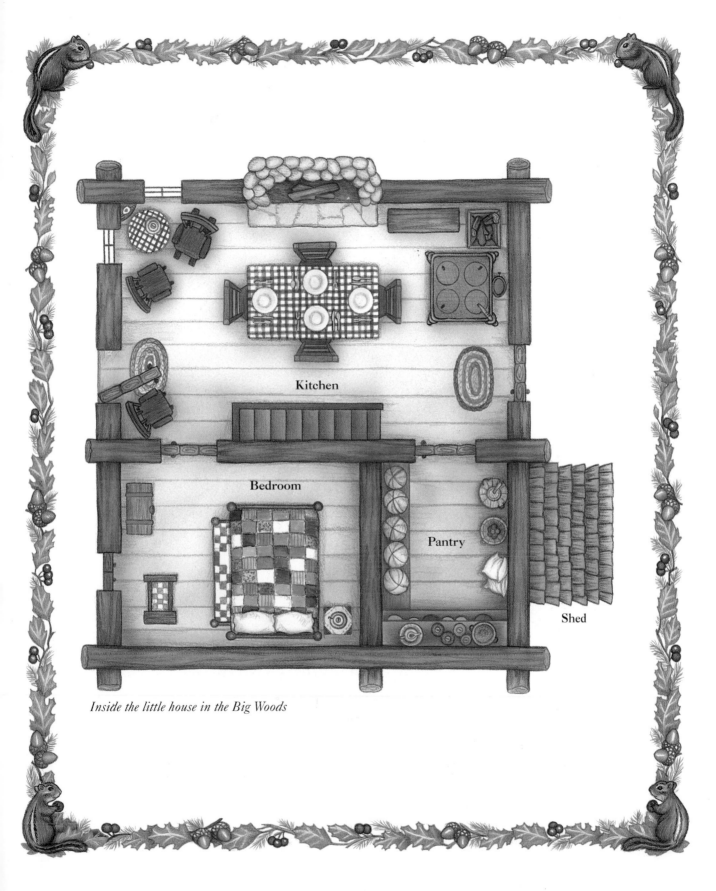

Kitchen

Bedroom

Pantry

Shed

Inside the little house in the Big Woods

Despite all the hard work they had to do, Laura and her family always found time to have fun, too. At night, Pa would tell Laura and Mary stories about his own childhood. Sometimes he would play some tunes on his fiddle before bedtime. Pa played hymns and folk songs, dances and marches. He played happy songs like "Pop! Goes the Weasel" and melancholy songs like "Auld Lang Syne."

The Ingalls family celebrated happy times with their relatives. Ma's sister and Pa's brother, who were married to each other, spent Christmas in the Big Woods with the Ingallses. Pa had carved a beautiful bracket for Ma's cherished china shepherdess. The bracket and the shepherdess would travel with the Ingallses to all their little houses and were a symbol of the constancy of their home life no matter where they lived. Laura also received a special gift—a rag doll with curly yarn hair. Laura named her doll Charlotte, and like Ma's shepherdess, Charlotte would go to all the little houses too.

The first Little House book ends after a whole year has passed. Autumn has come again to the Big Woods. Harvesting has begun, and soon snow will cover the fields and the garden and the paths, but Laura is safe and cozy and comfortable in the little house with Ma and Pa and Mary and Carrie.

The General Store

Laura could have looked for weeks
and not seen all the things that were in that store. She had not
known there were so many things in the world.

Ma and Pa built or made just about everything in the little house in the Big Woods, from the log cabin itself and the furniture in it to all their clothes, quilts, and sheets. They grew most of their food and even made their own soap.

Ma and Pa could not make everything they needed in the little house, though; some things they had to buy. So once in a while, Pa would go into town to the general store to buy what the family needed. One time, he took the whole family. It was a special occasion, and Laura always remembered her first trip to town.

The town they went to was Pepin, Wisconsin. It was about seven miles from the little house, and it was right beside a wide spot in the Mississippi River called

Lake Pepin. It took about two hours to get to town in the wagon. Coming back took a little longer, because the road was uphill nearly all the way.

To buy things at the store, Pa traded the furs he collected during the winter by setting out traps for various animals—otter, beaver, mink, even bear. He took the furs to the storekeeper, and the storekeeper gave Pa either money or store credit for them.

A general store when Laura was growing up was part grocery store, part hardware store, and part feed store. Goods came to the Pepin general store by riverboats from different parts of the country. There were bolts of cloth, sacks of sugar, and plugs of tobacco that traveled north on riverboats from southern cities like Memphis and New Orleans. From the mills in the northern states came iron and steel goods such as plows, guns, axes, hammers, nails, hoes, buckets, pots, and cookstoves. The general store also carried kitchen utensils and dishware made of tin or china, glassware, and silverware. Skeins of yarn, spools of thread, ribbons, lace and other trimmings, buttons, thimbles, needles, and scissors were available for home sewing. There were candle molds, candlewicks, glass lamps, and kerosene to burn in the lamps. Sometimes there would be a few books, such as *Millbank*, a novel that Uncle Tom Quiner, Ma's youngest brother, gave the Ingallses, and magazines like

Godey's Lady's Book. Schoolchildren bought their schoolbooks, slates, pens, and pencils at the general store.

Groceries were also part of the general store's stock. A general store would have barrels of salted meats and fish, pickles and crackers; lard, flour, salt, and jars of colorful candy. Boxes of tea and big bags of coffee beans were on hand. The storekeeper could roast the coffee beans and grind them in the store or sell the green coffee beans for the settlers to roast and grind at home. There were big boxes of spices, too. The store- keeper would weigh what- ever the customer wanted and

put it in a paper sack or wrap it in paper and string.

Most of the fruits in the store were dried, but sometimes there would be fresh fruit, such as bananas or oranges or grapefruit. Canned goods were just beginning to become available in stores when Laura made her first trip to the Pepin general store and became widely available after 1880.

There was some ready-made clothing in the general store, but most people on the frontier made their own clothes. That is why the general store had such a large supply of cloth on hand for Ma to look at. Calico, a popular material for clothes, sold for about fifteen cents a yard at that time.

Unless a shoemaker came around regularly, people would buy their leather shoes and boots at the store for a dollar or two a pair. They could buy gloves, machine-knit stockings, hoops and corsets, hats, and perhaps some heavy coats, too.

Patent medicines that claimed to cure all kinds of diseases could also be bought at a general store. The price of these medicines ranged from twenty-five cents to a dollar a bottle. Most of these were not effective, however, and some were even dangerous. Ma usually made her own medicines from roots and herbs she gathered herself.

A general store was crowded with merchandise stacked on the counters and shelves, piled on the floor, and hanging from the walls and rafters. Sometimes there was even a post office tucked into a corner of the store! Even though it was crowded, a general store always had room for people to gather. Often the men would sit and talk around the big iron stove that heated the store in winter. They passed along news from families they knew and talked about the politics of the day. It was not considered proper for girls and women to linger in public places, however, so they would leave the store as soon as their buying was done.

The general store began to fade out around the turn of the century, when department stores and mail-order houses like Montgomery Ward and Sears, Roebuck and Co. became a more convenient and popular way for people who did not live in a town to shop. The first Christmas gift Laura and Almanzo exchanged after they got married— a set of glass dishware—came from a Montgomery Ward catalogue. Although there are not as many general stores now as there were when Laura was growing up, some small towns still have a general store where people can buy a range of items and gather to talk about the day's news.

Ma's Clove Apple

Aunt Eliza had brought Ma a large red apple stuck full of cloves.
How good it smelled! And it would not spoil, for so many
cloves would keep it sound and sweet.

Aunt Eliza was Ma's sister, and her husband, Uncle Peter, was Pa's brother. They lived about twelve miles away in the Big Woods, and they came to celebrate Christmas at the little house. Aunt Eliza gave Ma a clove apple as a Christmas gift.

To make a clove apple you will need:

1 large red apple, very firm

½ cup whole cloves

Toothpick (optional)

1. Press the sharp point of each clove into the apple. Push it in until only the head of the clove shows. You may need a toothpick to help you get started.

2. Continue until the whole apple is covered with cloves. You can make some designs on the apple with the cloves.

3. To display your apple, place it on a dish or in a bowl out of direct sunlight.

You can also make clove oranges and clove lemons the same way you make clove apples.

Molasses-on-Snow Candy

One morning she boiled molasses and sugar together until they
made a thick syrup, and Pa brought in two pans of clean, white snow from outdoors.
Laura and Mary each had a pan, and Pa and Ma showed them how
to pour the dark syrup in little streams onto the snow.
They made circles, and curlicues, and squiggledy things, and these
hardened at once and were candy.

Before Christmas, Ma spent many hours making good things to eat, including molasses-on-snow candy. Laura and Mary helped Ma make the candy and were allowed to eat one piece each. The rest they saved for Christmas Day, when Aunt Eliza, Uncle Peter, and the cousins came to visit.

To make molasses-on-snow candy, you will need:

1 cup molasses
1 cup brown sugar
Fresh clean snow (or finely
  crushed ice)
Measuring cup
Large pot

Spoon
Candy thermometer or cup of
  cold water
Shallow pan about 9" x 13"
Clean tea towel or waxed paper

1. Mix the molasses and sugar together in the large pot and boil until the mixture reaches the "hard crack" stage on the thermometer or until a drop of the mixture dropped into the cold water forms a hard ball and cracks.

2. Remove the syrup from the heat. *Be careful—the syrup is very, very hot!*

3. Scoop fresh, clean snow into the shallow pan. You can also use finely crushed ice instead of snow.

4. Dribble a spoonful of syrup onto the snow or ice in "circles, and curlicues, and squiggledy things." Make lots of different shapes.

5. When the syrup turns hard and becomes candy, lift it off the snow and place it on the tea towel or waxed paper to dry.

Little House on the Prairie

Pa and Ma and Mary and Laura and Baby Carrie left their little house in the
Big Woods of Wisconsin. They drove away and left it lonely and empty in the clearing
among the big trees, and they never saw that little house again.
They were going to the Indian country.

LITTLE HOUSE ON THE PRAIRIE tells of Laura and her family's journey by covered wagon from the Big Woods of Wisconsin to a new home on the Kansas prairie.

Pa wanted to move to a part of the country where there were fewer people competing for game and water, and fewer tree stumps and tree seedlings crowding his fields. So he sold their Big Woods land, and the family headed south in their covered wagon. After the cozy, comfortable life in the Big Woods of Wisconsin, close to family and friends, the Ingallses were now on their own.

It was a long and difficult journey. The loaded wagon rolled slowly over the rutted roads through Minnesota, Iowa, Missouri, and eastern Kansas with Jack, the brindle bulldog, trotting alongside it. They had to cross raging rivers and once almost lost Jack. But the wagon trip was also an adventure that allowed them to see new country every day.

When the Ingallses finally crossed into Kansas, they began looking for a place to settle. The town of Independence was being built even as they passed through. Many of the "buildings" were made of hay, so eager were the people

The way to the prairie

to put up some kind of shelter there and claim a parcel of land. Pa drove the wagon past the town and out farther onto the prairie until he found a piece of land that seemed just right. There was a creek flowing through it, and the trees that grew along the creek could provide logs for building and for firewood. More important to Pa, there were wide-open fields of prairie grass with no big trees to cut down or plow around.

Right away, Pa "claimed" the land by building a house on it. There was a lot to do to turn the new land into a home and a farm. With the help of neighbors, Pa first built a small one-room log cabin, and then he built a log barn for the horses. Afterward he dug a deep well near the cabin so the family would have fresh water to drink. Then he plowed through the thick prairie grass to make fields for the spring crops.

Life was not always easy on the prairie for the Ingallses. They had to fight prairie fires and sickness. The whole family was struck with "fever 'n' ague," which we know today as malaria. The mosquitoes that thrived along the creeks nearby carried the disease. Fortunately, a doctor who lived on the prairie was able to treat them. His name was Dr. George Tann, and he worked among the Osage Indians who lived by the creeks and rivers near the little house, and who owned the land the Ingalls family lived on.

Despite these difficulties, Laura and her family liked living on the prairie.

Inside the little house on the prairie

Well

Laura and Pa especially loved the open sky and wide stretches of grasslands. However, the United States government had not yet paid the Osage for their land, and the Osage were angry. Kansas settlers like Pa were worried there might be a war, but one of the Osage leaders, Soldat du Chêne, convinced his people not to fight the settlers. Instead, the Osage left their camps and moved south into Oklahoma Territory. Laura watched the long line of Osage ride past the little house on their way to Oklahoma Territory. Because the land the Ingalls family lived on still belonged to the Osage tribe, though, they too had to leave. *Little House on the Prairie* ends with Laura and her family traveling by covered wagon once again and looking for another place to live.

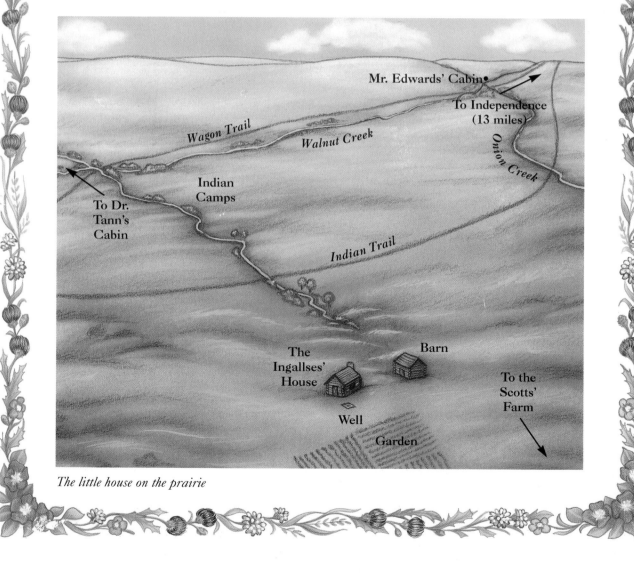

The little house on the prairie

Covered Wagons

Everything from the little house was in the wagon,
except the beds and tables and chairs. They did not need to take these,
because Pa could always make new ones.

In 1869, when the Ingallses moved to Indian Territory, the most common way for a family to travel long distances was by covered wagon. Ma and Pa were used to trips by covered wagon. Pa had traveled by wagon many times since he was a teenager, first from New York State to Illinois, then to Concord, Wisconsin. He and Ma had moved to the Big Woods from Concord by wagon.

A covered wagon had to be constructed very carefully. It had to be strong enough to carry everything from mattresses to pots and pans and still be lightweight enough for the horses or oxen to pull. It also needed to be watertight so that the contents of the wagon would stay dry when it rained or when the travelers were crossing rivers. Most wagons were made of well-seasoned oak boards. A typical wagon was about four feet wide by ten feet long. The depth of the wagon box would vary, depending on what the family or traveler planned to take on the trip. Pa's wagon had a seat across the front where he and Ma sat, but some wagons did not have a seat. Instead, the driver would walk alongside the horses or oxen and guide them.

The wagon wheels were made of wood and had strips of iron around the edges to keep them from wearing out too fast. The front wheels were smaller than the back wheels so that the wagon could take sharp turns more easily, without danger of tipping over.

The wagon was covered with a large piece of canvas or sailcloth that was laid over five or six arched "bows" of green hickory wood. The ends of the bows fit into brackets on the sides of the wagon. There were strings attached to the canvas cover that could be tied to each bow to hold the cover down tight. There were also drawstrings at the front and back that could open and close the cover. Some people oiled the canvas to make it water-repellent.

The Ingalls family would have had to pack many things in the wagon for their long journey to Kansas. First of all, they needed plenty of food for the trip. Pa could always hunt for game along the way, and they could buy supplies in any town they might pass through. The farther out on the prairie they went, though, the fewer towns there would be, and the supplies would be scarcer and more expensive.

Most wagon travelers packed about a hundred pounds each of flour, cornmeal, beans, and sugar, and smaller sacks or cans of salt, tea, and coffee. They usually took bacon or salt pork on the trail because it kept well. Some travelers might also take jerky, which was dried beef or venison. Fruits and potatoes were usually dried, too, so they would not spoil, would be lighter in weight, and would not take up so much room.

Feed for the horses had to be packed, too. The horses would eat grass along the way, but they also needed grain for protein in order to keep their muscles strong for pulling the heavy wagon. A barrel of water was usually tied to the outside of the wagon so that horses and passengers would have drinking water if they could not find a clean stream or spring along the trail.

Kettles and pots and pans, kitchen knives, cooking forks, and spoons went into the wagon along with dishes and silverware. Some of the bigger pots could be hung on the outside of the wagon, but they would have to be lashed on tightly so that they would not rattle and frighten the horses. Breakable things were wrapped in clothing or linens or sometimes were placed in the sacks of flour or meal to cushion them. Pa's fiddle and Ma's china shepherdess were wrapped in quilts and carefully set in a safe place in the back of the wagon.

Although many travelers packed furniture in their covered wagons, Laura's family did not take furniture in their wagon, because Pa could make new beds, tables, and chairs. They did take straw mattresses, though, and sheets and quilts. Mary and Laura sat on the mattresses while the wagon moved, and the whole family slept on them in the wagon at night.

Traveling by covered wagon was very slow, because the wagon had so much in it. Horses or oxen could not pull the heavily loaded wagon very fast or very far at one time. Twenty miles a day was about all a covered wagon could go before the animals had to rest. If the road was very bad or there were lots of hills to climb, the animals could not even go that far.

The roads at the time the Ingalls family traveled were very rough. They were generally just dirt roads with deep ruts from the many wagons traveling the same road. When it rained, the dirt would turn to sticky, heavy mud. This made it nearly impossible for the horses or oxen to pull the wagon. The travelers would often have to stop and wait for the roads to dry out. Sometimes this would be a day or two, but sometimes it could take weeks.

How did Pa know which way to go to get to Indian Territory? There were no road maps such as we have today, and the roads were not always marked with signs. Pa may have had a trail book to help him. These handbooks were written by trail guides or soldiers to help pioneers find their way. They had directions from a major starting point, such as St. Paul, Minnesota, to a final destination,

usually westward. A sketchy map might be included in these guidebooks. The directions were general and identified landmarks and fords, good camping spots and watering holes, road conditions, and types of terrain.

The days of the covered wagon came to an end as more railroads were built across the country. Travelers could go to more and more places by train, and they could get there much faster and more comfortably, too.

Hide the Thimble

In the cozy, firelit house Mary and Laura helped Ma with the work. Then they sewed quilt-patches. They played Patty Cake with Carrie, and they played Hide the Thimble.

During the dark and cold days of winter on the Kansas prairie, Laura and Mary could not stay outside for long. So they played all kinds of games indoors, instead, including Hide the Thimble. A thimble is a little metal cup that fits on top of your finger when you are sewing. It keeps the needle from hurting your fingertip as you push the needle through the fabric.

To play Hide the Thimble, you will need:

A thimble (or other small object)   *One or more friends*

1. Choose who will hide the thimble first.

2. All the other players close their eyes and count to ten slowly while the thimble hider finds a good spot to hide the thimble.

3. Then the players open their eyes and look for the thimble, while the thimble hider counts to fifty.

4. The first person to find the thimble is the one to hide it next. If no one finds the thimble in time, the same thimble hider hides it again in a new place.

Mary and Laura's Nine-Patch Quilt Squares

*Mary and Laura stayed close by the fire,
sewing their nine-patch quilt blocks . . . and hearing
the wet sound of the rain.*

Mary and Laura began their nine-patch quilt squares back in the little house in the Big Woods. Mary was six years old then, and Laura was four. They kept working on the quilt squares whenever there was time. The nine-patch pattern is named for the nine small squares or patches that are sewn together into a bigger square with three patches on each side and one in the middle. It is a simple, easy patchwork pattern, because all the squares are the same size and they are sewn in straight rows.

To make your own nine-patch quilt square, you will need:

5 squares (each 4" x 4") printed
    cotton fabric
4 squares (each 4" x 4") contrast-
    ing printed cotton fabric

Needle and thread
Scissors

1. Lay the nine squares of fabric out in a square as shown, alternating squares so that no like ones are next to each other.

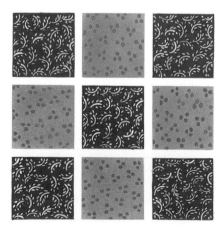

2. Sew three squares together into a strip, with ¼" seam allowances and repeat until you have three strips.

3. Sew the three strips together into a square. This is one nine-patch quilt square.

4. Hem the edges and use the square for a doll blanket. Or you can sew a 12" square of fabric onto the back around three sides, stuff with stuffing, and sew up the fourth side, to make a small pillow for your bed.

To make a whole quilt like Mary and Laura's, you would need to make 32 nine-patch squares and sew them all together!

Laura's
Heart-Shaped Cakes

*Mary and Laura pulled out two small packages. They unwrapped them,
and each found a little heart-shaped cake. Over their delicate brown tops was sprinkled
white sugar. The sparkling grains lay like tiny drifts of snow.*

The Ingallses' neighbor, Mr. Edwards, swam across a rain-swollen creek in the freezing cold to bring Mary and Laura their presents from Santa Claus—shiny new tin cups, sticks of peppermint candy, a penny apiece, and delicate heart-shaped cakes. Laura and Mary thought the cakes were almost too pretty to eat.

To make heart-shaped cakes, you will need:

½ cup butter or margarine,
   softened
2 tablespoons granulated sugar
¼ teaspoon vanilla
1¼ cups all-purpose flour
Granulated sugar for sprinkling
Measuring cup and spoons
Large mixing bowl
Mixing spoon

Floured board
Rolling pin (optional)
Heart-shaped cookie cutter,
   about 2"–3" across
Cookie sheet
Pot holder
Wide spatula
Wire rack

1. Preheat the oven to 325°.

2. Beat the butter, sugar, and vanilla together until the mixture is light and fluffy.

3. Stir in the flour.

4. On a floured board, pat or roll the dough out into a circle about ⅓" thick.

5. Cut out shapes with the cookie cutter.

6. Gather the leftover scraps into a ball. Pat or roll the ball into a circle, and cut more cakes.

7. Sprinkle the tops of the cakes with granulated sugar.

8. Put the cakes on the cookie sheet and bake them for about 15–20 minutes, until they are lightly browned.

9. Take the cakes out of the oven and sprinkle more granulated sugar on the tops.

10. Carefully remove the cakes with a spatula to a wire rack to cool.

This recipe makes about 12 heart-shaped cakes.

Farmer Boy

A farmer depends on himself, and the land and the weather.

FARMER BOY is the story of nine-year-old Almanzo Wilder, who would one day become Laura Ingalls's husband. Laura wrote this story about Almanzo when they had been married for nearly fifty years.

Almanzo's childhood was very different from Laura's. He did not travel from place to place by covered wagon, and he did not live on the frontier. Instead, he lived on the same farm in upstate New York from the time he was born until he was a teenager. The farm was large and productive, and the land was free of stumps. Almanzo's life was, in many ways, easier and more comfortable than Laura's. It was certainly more predictable.

During the day, Almanzo and his brothers and sisters attended the one-room school close to their farm. Each Sunday, the family drove by horse and buggy into the nearby town of Malone for church. They also went to town on special occasions—for the Independence Day celebration and the annual county fair. When Almanzo was nine years old, he took a milk-fed pumpkin that he had raised all by himself to the county fair. It was so big and so delicious that Almanzo won first prize!

The Wilders bought many of their supplies in town. However, there were still peddlers and craftsmen who traveled around the countryside selling their wares from wagons. Almanzo always looked forward to the tin peddler's visit in

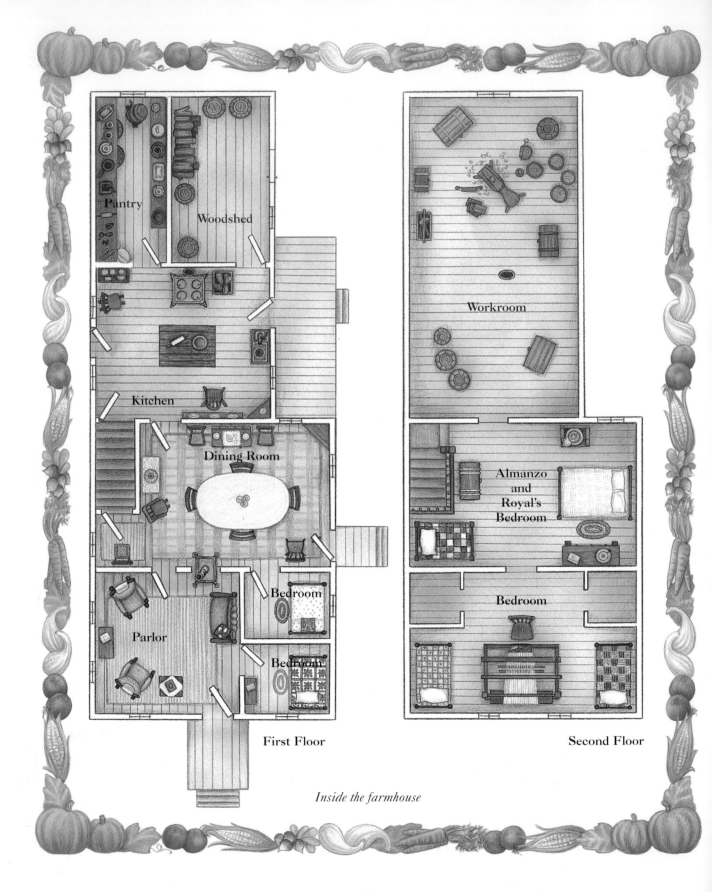

Pantry

Woodshed

Kitchen

Dining Room

Parlor

Bedroom

Bedroom

Workroom

Almanzo
and
Royal's
Bedroom

Bedroom

First Floor

Second Floor

Inside the farmhouse

the spring, when Mother traded rags for pots and pans, and to the shoemaker's visit in the fall, when Almanzo would have new shoes made.

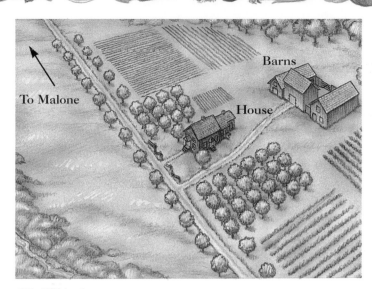

The Wilder farm

During part of the year, Almanzo went to school. The school was a mile away from the Wilder farmhouse, and Almanzo walked there and back, even in the snow. When Almanzo was not in school, he helped his father and his big brother, Royal, with many of the chores around the farm. Having such a large farm meant there was always work to do. There were fields to plant and harvest and orchards to tend. There were cattle, oxen, horses, and sheep to care for. Father even gave Almanzo his own little calves for his ninth birthday, and Almanzo trained them to wear a yoke and pull a sled so that he could help carry firewood and other supplies around the farm. Almanzo also helped his mother and sisters with the chores in the house and garden.

Almanzo worked so hard that he was always hungry, and *Farmer Boy* is full of the many delicious foods Almanzo relished. At Christmastime, the Wilders celebrated with "the best dinner of the whole year." Mother roasted a whole little pig and a goose with stuffing. There were bowls of gravy, and potatoes, cranberry jelly, turnips, candied carrots, parsnips, squash, and fried apples'n'onions, Almanzo's favorite dish. For dessert, there were pies and fruitcake.

Almanzo loved farming, he loved working outside, and he especially loved horses. When he was almost ten, the town wheelwright, who made and repaired wagons and buggies, offered Almanzo an apprenticeship. Almanzo turned down the offer because he knew, even then, that he wanted to be a farmer.

The County Fair

*This morning the roads were lively with people driving to
the Fair, and in Malone the crowds were thicker than they had been on Independence Day.
All around the Fair Grounds were acres of wagons and buggies, and people were
clustered like flies. Flags were flying and the band was playing.*

Every fall when Almanzo was growing up, a fair was held in Malone, the county seat of Franklin County, New York. Other fairs were held in other counties throughout the United States. The county fair was the occasion when everyone in a particular community could come together and see what their neighbors had been working on during the year. Farm families brought their best animals—sheep, horses, cows, oxen, pigs, and poultry—to be judged. They also brought fruits, vegetables, and flowers from their gardens to see who had grown the biggest and the best. There were competitions for the best household manufactures: butter and cheese, maple sugar and honey, and home-baked bread. There were contests for quilts, blankets, carpets, straw hats, and home-spun yarn. The "fancy work" category included shell work, wax flowers, crocheting, worsted work, leatherwork, hair-flower wreaths (made from human hair!), and feather flowers. Making flowers from hair and feathers was a popular hobby in the nineteenth century, and many people decorated their homes with them. There were contests for farm machinery, buggies and sleighs, harness and saddle making, black-smithing, and barrel making. There was even a prize for dentistry! Whoever won first prize in each category was awarded a ribbon and sometimes money, which ranged from a dollar for the best needlework to twenty dollars for the best pure-bred bull.

Until the early 1800's, there were no county fairs. Farmers simply brought their produce and animals into the nearest town to sell in a farmers' market. On market day, the farmers sold their goods from their wagons or from temporary stands set up in a vacant lot. Then, in 1811, the Berkshire Agricultural Society in Massachusetts was formed, and it sponsored the very first "country fair." It was the model for county fairs that have been held ever since. That first fair boasted exhibitions of farm animals, demonstrations of farm machinery, contests for all kinds of domestic skills, and plenty of fiddle and banjo playing. There were also horse races, dances, parades, and political speeches. The fair was so successful that many other towns across the country began to organize their own fairs.

The first Franklin County fair was held in October 1820. About $100 in prizes were awarded that year. The Franklin County Fair that Laura describes in *Farmer Boy* took place in 1866, when Almanzo was nine years old. It was held at the fairgrounds a little east of Malone, and it is still held there today! When Almanzo was growing up, the local people came to the fair by horse and buggy, and tourists came in from miles around by train. The fair lasted for three days—Tuesday, Wednesday, and Thursday. The exhibits were displayed from the first day, and the judging was held on Wednesday. Prizes were awarded at the end of the day. On Thursday the winning animals were paraded around the fairgrounds for the crowd to admire. While admiring the exhibits and watching the parades, fairgoers would sip on lemonade or apple cider and snack on the homemade cookies and other good things to eat that they could buy at the food stands all around the fair grounds. Or they could watch the horse races, which were an important and popular part of county fairs. Almanzo went to the grandstand with Father to watch the races. The race he saw was memorable because an Indian joined the race and ran as fast as the winning horse!

County fairs have changed very little in the last hundred years. Even with the addition of rides, sideshows, and other amusements at some of the fairs over the years, their main purpose is still to provide a chance for communities to get together and admire the best of their local crops, animals, and handiwork.

Fried Apples 'n' Onions

Almanzo said that what he liked most in the world was fried apples'n'onions.

All morning, Almanzo had been helping Father stack big blocks of ice in the ice-house. At the noon meal, Mother served a big bowl of Almanzo's favorite dish, fried apples'n'onions, accompanied by roast beef and gravy, mashed potatoes, creamed carrots, and boiled turnips, and birds'-nest pudding for dessert.

To make fried apples'n'onions, you will need:

2 tablespoons bacon fat or oil
1 medium onion, peeled and cut into
  1" chunks
4 tart cooking apples, washed, cored,
  and cut into 1" chunks

1 to 2 tablespoons brown sugar
Crumbled cooked bacon (optional)
Measuring spoons
Large skillet or dutch oven with cover
Mixing spoon

1. Heat the fat in the skillet over medium heat.

2. Carefully add the onions and cook until they start to soften, about 5 minutes.

3. Add the apples, cook 1 minute, cover, and cook 3 or 4 minutes more.

4. Stir occasionally so the apples cook evenly.

5. Uncover and sprinkle the apples'n'onions with brown sugar and/or crumbled bacon if you like. Serve hot.

This recipe makes 4 servings.

Homemade Butter

*In the whitewashed cellar the big wooden barrel churn stood on its
wooden legs, half full of cream. Almanzo turned the handle, and the churn rocked.
Inside it the cream went chug! splash, chug! splash.*

There were many varieties of butter churns. Almanzo's churn was a barrel turned on its side and placed on rockers. As the churn rocked back and forth, the cream inside sloshed around and eventually made butter.

If you would like to make butter, here is a simple way to do it without a churn. To make butter, you will need:

1 pint heavy cream   *A quart-size jar with a*
Slotted spoon   *tight-fitting lid*

1. Pour the cream into the jar. Screw the lid on tight.

2. Shake the jar until the butter forms. You will know butter is forming when the cream thickens and starts to form a ball. This may take a while, so don't tire yourself out shaking the jar too hard.

3. Scoop the butter out of the jar and drain it on a tea towel.

4. Squeeze the butter inside the towel to get the remaining liquid out.

5. Form the butter into a pretty shape, put it on a plate, and chill it in the refrigerator until you are ready to eat it.

The remaining liquid is buttermilk. You can use buttermilk to cook with, or you can drink it.

Pulled Molasses Candy

They all pulled candy. They pulled it into long strands,
and doubled the strands, and pulled again. Every
time they doubled it, they took a bite.

Almanzo's mother and father visited Uncle Andrew for a week, leaving Almanzo, Royal, Eliza Jane, and Alice to take care of the house while they were gone. Without their parents around, Almanzo and his brother and sisters decided to do whatever they felt like doing, and one of the first things they did was make pulled molasses candy.

To make pulled molasses candy, you will need:

4 tablespoons butter or margarine	*Wooden spoon*
1 cup brown sugar	*Candy thermometer or cup of*
¼ cup molasses	* cold water*
Extra butter for buttering your	*Buttered platter*
* hands*	*Kitchen scissors*
Measuring cup and spoons	*Airtight container*
Large saucepan	

1. Combine the butter, brown sugar, and molasses in the saucepan.

2. Set over medium-high heat and bring the mixture to a boil. Turn the heat down but keep the mixture boiling.

3. Stir the mixture until it reaches 250° on the candy thermometer or forms a hard ball when a few drops are dropped into cold water. This will take about 20 minutes.

4. Carefully pour the hot mixture onto the buttered platter and let it cool at least 10 minutes until you can handle it without burning your hands. *Be extremely careful—the mixture will be very, very hot when you pour it out!*

5. Butter your hands well and pull off a handful of the molasses mixture.

6. Stretch it as far as you can without breaking the strand, fold it back together, stretch it again, over and over, until it begins to turn pale and creamy.

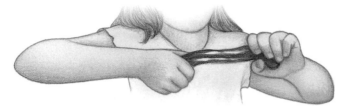

7. Stretch the candy into long ropes about ½" thick and cut the ropes into 1" pieces.

8. Let the pieces cool before you eat them. Store in an airtight container. This recipe makes about 50 pieces of candy.

On the Banks of Plum Creek

Laura went under those singing flowers into the dugout. It was one room, all white.
The earth walls had been smoothed and whitewashed. The earth floor was smooth and hard.

ON THE BANKS OF PLUM CREEK begins with the end of the Ingallses' long journey by covered wagon. They had traveled from Indian Territory in Kansas to settle near Walnut Grove, Minnesota.

This time, there was no dispute over the ownership of the land. The Ingallses bought a farm from Mr. Hanson, a Swedish immigrant, and they moved into his tiny dugout on the eastern bank of Plum Creek. After the Ingallses had moved into the one-room dugout, Mary and Laura spent the rest of the summer exploring their new surroundings. They swam in Plum Creek and climbed to the top of the flat tableland nearby. They played on the big gray rock they found on the prairie beyond the dugout. They picked juicy plums from the bushes along Plum Creek for Ma to dry in the hot summer sun.

The family spent the winter in the little dugout, which, with its thick sod walls, kept them warm and dry. In the spring, Pa built a house on the other side of Plum Creek. Laura called it "the wonderful house." It was made of sawn boards Pa bought, not logs, as in their previous little houses, and it had three rooms with glass windows. Pa even bought a brand-new cookstove for Ma. He bought the boards and stove on credit, confident that once his wheat crop was harvested, he could pay the money he owed.

The way to Plum Creek

Now that they lived close to a town, Mary and Laura could go to school. They walked the two miles into Walnut Grove and the two miles back home every day. They made some new friends and met a girl named Nellie Oleson, who was rude and mean to everyone, especially to Laura. Ma told Laura to be polite, and Laura was—to Nellie's face, at least. But Laura also found a way to get even with Nellie. Once, when they were wading in Plum Creek, Laura steered Nellie into a spot where her feet and legs were soon covered with black, slimy leeches!

The Ingallses went to church in Walnut Grove on Sundays. Their minister was the Reverend Alden, who liked to call Laura and Mary his "little country girls." Laura saw her first Christmas tree in the Walnut Grove church. There was one tree for the whole community. It was not an evergreen tree, like those we use now, but a small tree with bare branches. It was decorated with green tissue paper and strings of popcorn. There

Plum Creek

Inside the dugout

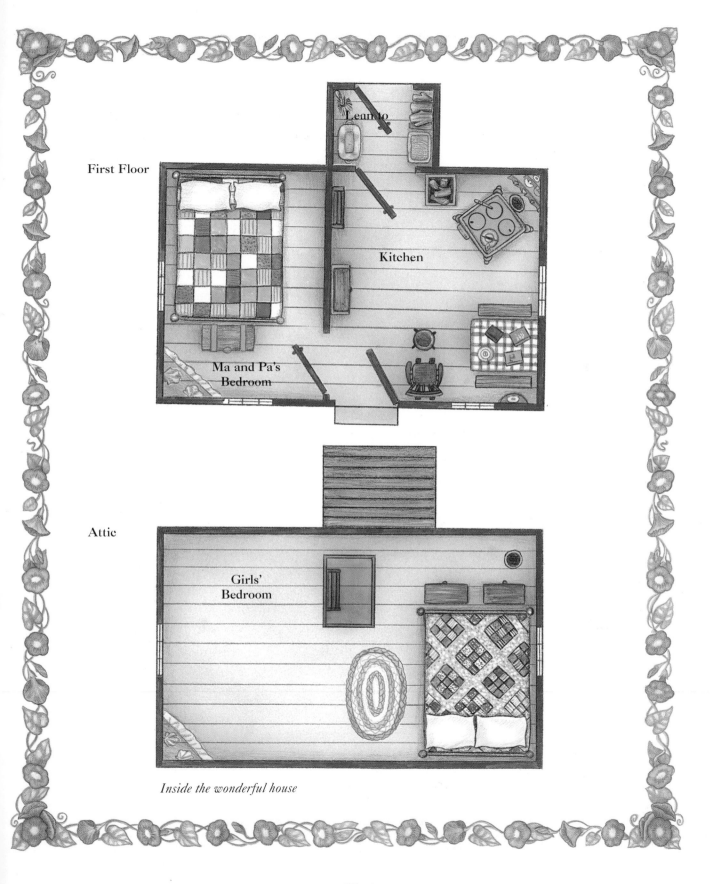

First Floor

Lean-to

Kitchen

Ma and Pa's
Bedroom

Attic

Girls'
Bedroom

Inside the wonderful house

were gifts and net bags of candy hanging on the branches, and more gifts were piled at the base of the tree. The gifts were handed out in church. Laura was given mittens and a little china jewel box with a tiny tea set on top. Then she was given a fur muff and cape that were even nicer than Nellie's!

Such a joyous Christmas celebration was a bright spot in a difficult year for the Ingalls family and the other farmers of Walnut Grove. Their hopes for a good crop that summer had been crushed when clouds of grasshoppers descended all over the southern part of Minnesota. The grasshoppers ate every bit of wheat; then they laid eggs that would hatch the next year. In a matter of days, the Ingallses and other families for miles around lost two years' worth of crops to the grasshoppers. In order to pay for the new house and to buy new supplies, Pa had to walk many miles back to eastern Minnesota and help with the harvesting there. He could not even afford the few dollars it would have cost to take the train. The book ends with another Christmas celebration. This time there were no gifts for Laura and Mary, but they got something even better: the safe return of Pa, who had been caught in a blizzard for four long days.

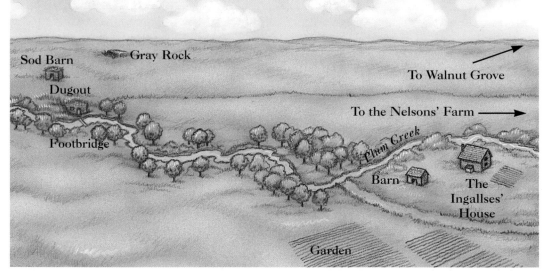

On the banks of Plum Creek

Housekeeping on the Prairie

"Come on," Laura told Mary. "We've got the work to do."
They washed and wiped the dishes. They shook the snow off their bedcovers
and made their bed. They warmed again by the stove, then they polished it,
and Mary cleaned the woodbox while Laura swept the floors.

Housekeeping on the frontier was hard work. There were no vacuum cleaners or kitchen appliances. Everything had to be done by hand. Living in houses with dirt floors, smoky fireplaces, woodstoves, and dim lighting made the work even more difficult. It took all week just to keep up with the cleaning, washing, ironing, mending, and cooking. Most of the household chores were done by the women and girls in the family. After the breakfast dishes were washed and the beds were made, it was time to do the day's special chore.

In the Ingallses' little houses, as in most frontier households, every day of the week had its own "proper work." Monday's clothes washing was probably the most arduous chore of the week. First, bucket after bucket of water had to be brought in from the spring or the well to fill a big iron pot on the cookstove. A large supply of wood had to be chopped and ready in the woodbox to keep the fire going in the stove, because the water needed to be heated and kept boiling during the washing.

The white things would be washed first, then the colored things, so that the dyes in the colored clothes would not spoil the white ones. The clothes were scrubbed by hand on a ribbed scrubbing board in the washtub with strong homemade soap.

After the clothes were scrubbed, they were boiled for about half an hour, and stirred constantly with a long stick. They were then lifted out of the hot, soapy water with the stick into another tub, and the water was squeezed out. When all the clothes were washed, the wash water was dumped outside. More buckets of fresh water were hauled in to heat on the stove for rinsing the clothes.

When all the clothes were rinsed and wrung out, they were hung up to dry. In summer, they could be hung outside in the sun and fresh air, but in winter, they would have to be hung inside the house, perhaps in the attic or a lean-to.

On Tuesday, the ironing board would be set up. The board was padded with a thick layer of blankets, and the blankets were covered with a clean sheet. Sometimes it was laid across two chair backs, or one end was rested on the dinner table and the other end on a chair back. Meanwhile, heavy flatirons were heating on the cookstove. When they were hot enough, the ironing could begin.

Everything the family wore was ironed, including underwear. The heat from the iron not only smoothed out the wrinkles, it also killed any germs and insect eggs that might still be in the clothes.

By Wednesday, the pioneer woman needed a good rest from the heavy labor of washing and ironing! Ma could sit in her rocker to do the mending. She could work on a new shirt for Pa or dresses for herself and the girls. Although the sewing machine had been available since the 1840's (powered by a treadle, not electricity), there were not many in the log cabins and dugouts on the prairie. Virtually everything the Ingalls family wore, as well as all their sheets, blankets, and other household linens, were made by hand. While the mothers sewed, their daughters, like Laura and Mary, practiced their stitching on scraps of cloth. These were called "samplers" because the girls stitched samples of various embroidery stitches on them. Laura made her first sampler when she was four years old. She and Mary also sewed little scraps of cloth into patchwork squares.

Thursday in the Ingalls household was churning day. When Mary and then Laura were about six years old, they could help churn the butter. After the cow was milked on Wednesday, the milk was set aside and allowed to rest, undisturbed, overnight. The cream rose to the top and Ma poured it into the churn.

In the lid of Ma's churn was a long handle with a flat piece of wood on the bottom. This was called a dasher, and it had to be moved up and down constantly through the cream until the butter formed a lump. Then the butter was scraped from the dasher and washed in clean water. It was salted so that it would not spoil too quickly and was packed into a crock to keep it cool. Ma liked to press some of her freshly churned butter into her wooden butter mold. The pats of butter came out with a pretty strawberry design on top.

Cleaning the cabin was Friday's work. In the log cabins or in the dugouts on the prairie, the women and girls would use a twig broom to sweep not only the floors but also the rough walls and ceilings. If a cabin had a wood floor, they scrubbed it with water, sand, and lye soap. They polished the iron stove and dusted the furniture. They cleaned the ashes out of the stove and fireplace and saved them to make soap or fertilizer. Once every spring and fall, they filled the bed ticks with fresh straw and washed all the quilts and blankets.

On Saturday, the baking for the week was done. The bread dough was mixed and then had to rise two or three times before it was baked. Several loaves were baked at a time in a big square baking pan. If there were enough eggs and butter on hand, the housewife might bake a cake. Pies were a very popular dessert on the prairie, too.

Sunday was always a well-deserved day of rest. Organized churches in the east sent itinerant preachers such as the Reverend Alden to establish churches in the new towns on the prairie. The Ingalls family went to church if they lived close enough to one, as they did in Walnut Grove. If they were in the Big Woods or on the prairie or traveling in the wagon, they would read the Bible, sing their favorite hymns, and spend the day quietly.

Thimble Pictures

*Ma gave her thimble to Laura, and Mary's thimble to Carrie, and
she showed them that pressing the thimbles into the frost on the windows
made perfect circles. They could make pictures on the windows.
With thimble-circles Laura made a Christmas tree. She made birds
flying. She made a log house with smoke coming out of the chimney.
She even made a roly-poly man and a roly-poly woman.*

During the long four-day blizzard, when Ma and the girls were waiting for Pa to come home, Ma showed Laura and Carrie how to make pretty designs on the frosty windowpanes of their house on Plum Creek.

To make thimble pictures, all you need is a thimble and a frosty windowpane. Press the thimble into the frost and make a design.

If you don't have a frosty windowpane to make thimble pictures on, you can press a thimble onto an ink pad and make thimble designs on paper. You can also put a thin layer of sugar, cornmeal, or sand in a shallow pan and make designs in the pan with the thimble. Shake the pan to erase the pictures and create new ones. If you don't have a thimble, try a bottle cap.

Star-edged Shelf Paper

Ma brought out two long strips of brown wrapping-paper that she had saved. She folded them, and she showed Mary and Laura how to cut tiny bits out of the folded paper with the scissors. When each unfolded her paper, there was a row of stars. Ma spread the paper on the shelves behind the stove. The stars hung over the edges of the shelves, and the light shone through them.

When Pa finished building the wonderful new house on the banks of Plum Creek, the star-edged shelf paper made the plain, unpainted shelves look nice.

To make star-edged shelf paper, you will need:

Paper from a supermarket bag or wrapping paper	*Pencil*
	Scissors

1. Make sure your paper is wide enough to hang over the edge of your shelf, and make sure it is as long as the shelf. Tape pieces of paper together if you need to.

2. Fold the strip of paper into ½" accordion pleats.

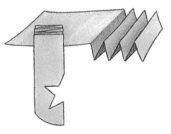

3. Cut out pieces according to the diagram. Carefully unfold the paper and smooth it out.

4. Fold the edge with the stars down so that the stars hang down over the edge of the shelf. Secure the paper on the shelf with pieces of tape if you want to.

Town Party Lemonade

*"Is your lemonade sweet enough?" Mrs. Oleson asked. So Laura knew
that it was lemonade in the glasses. She had never tasted anything like it.*

The lemons for the lemonade Laura tasted at Nellie's party would have
come by train to Walnut Grove all the way from Florida.

To make lemonade, you will need:

1 cup sugar	*Ice*	*Sharp knife*
1 cup boiling water	*Measuring cup*	*Bowl or juicer*
3 lemons	*Small bowl*	*Pitcher*
3 cups cold water	*Long-handled spoon*	*6 tall glasses*

1. Put the sugar into the small bowl and add the
boiling water; stir to dissolve the sugar. Set aside.

2. Roll the lemons on a kitchen counter or table
with your palm a few times to make them juicier.

3. Carefully cut the lemons in half.

4. Squeeze as much of the juice from the
lemons as you can into a bowl, or use a juicer if you
have one. Remove any seeds with a spoon.

5. Pour the juice into the pitcher.

6. Stir the sugar water into the lemon juice, then
add the cold water and stir.

7. Taste the lemonade to see if it is sweet
enough. If it isn't, add more sugar to taste.

8. Pour the lemonade over ice in tall glasses to
serve.

This recipe serves six.

By the Shores of Silver Lake

*There was a little starshine on Silver Lake, and all around it
stretched the black prairie, flat under the velvet-dark sky sparkling with stars.*

BY THE SHORES OF SILVER LAKE is the fifth book in the Little House series. It tells of the last major journey Laura and her family made together—this time to Dakota Territory. At the same time, the book tells the story of how a railroad was built across the Great Plains.

In the summer of 1879, Pa's sister Docia (her full name was Laura Ladocia) stopped by the Ingallses' house on Plum Creek. She was on her way west to join her husband, who was working for the Dakota Central Railroad, and she had a proposition for Pa. Would he be interested in a job with the railroad, too?

In the four years that had passed since grasshoppers had devastated the crops around the town of Walnut Grove, the Ingallses had suffered many more hardships. Several years of poor crops had left the family in debt. Mary had lost her sight in a terrible illness. One of the very few bright spots during those years was the birth of the Ingallses' fourth daughter, Grace.

After a long discussion with Ma, Pa decided to take the job with the railroad. He left the next day with Aunt Docia and spent the next few months as storekeeper and bookkeeper for the railroad. In early September, Ma and the girls left Walnut Grove on the train. This was the first time the girls had traveled by railroad. Pa met them with a horse and wagon and took them the rest of the way

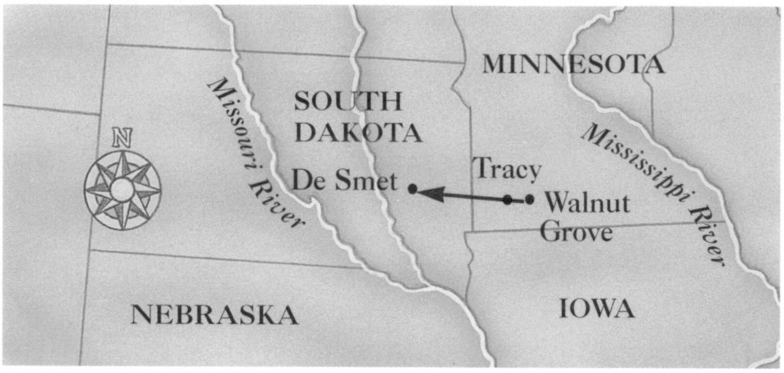

The way to Silver Lake

to the railroad camp. In a few days, they moved on with the railroad crew to set up a new camp about forty miles farther west.

For three months, the Ingalls family lived in a one-room shanty in the railroad camp by the shores of Silver Lake. The railroad men worked every day grading the bed for the rails. By December, the entire crew had left to spend the winter back east—all, that is, but the Ingallses. The railroad offered to pay Pa to stay in the Surveyors' House over the winter to guard the railroad's equipment and property.

This was a wonderful opportunity for the Ingalls family. They could live in a large, well-built house full of supplies, and not have to make another long trip. Pa would draw a salary, and he could find a homestead before the spring rush.

The Surveyors' House was the nicest house the Ingallses had lived in yet. To

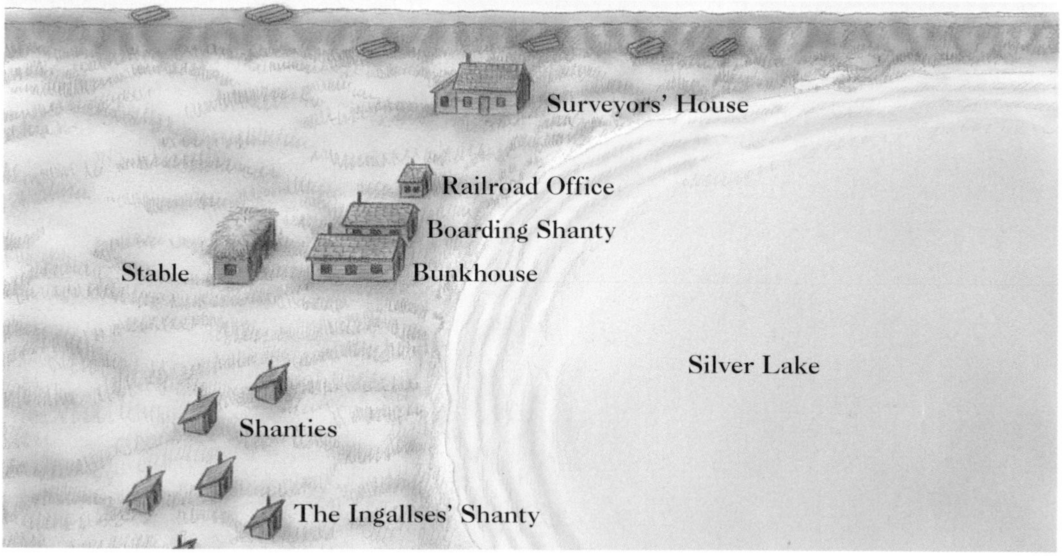

The railroad camp

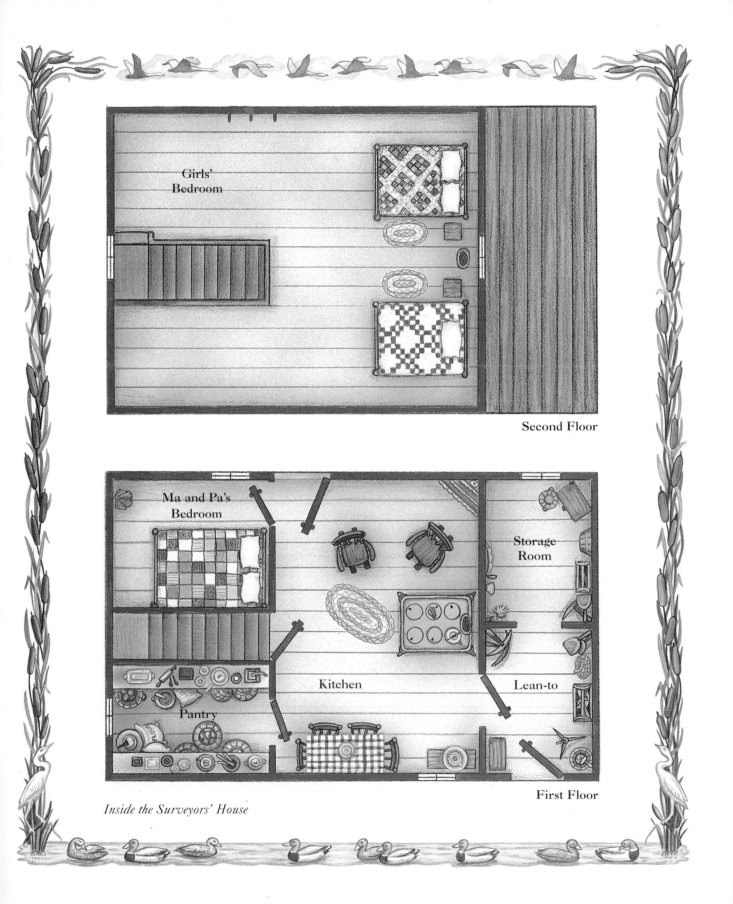

Girls' Bedroom

Second Floor

Ma and Pa's Bedroom

Storage Room

Pantry

Kitchen

Lean-to

First Floor

Inside the Surveyors' House

Laura, it seemed immense. There was a large living room, a bedroom, a pantry, and two storage rooms on the first floor, and there was an attic room that became a bedroom for Mary, Laura, and Carrie. The pantry was stocked with all sorts of canned goods, flour, sugar, coffee, crackers, and other luxuries. A big cookstove was already set up, and there was plenty of coal to last the winter.

The family spent a comfortable, happy winter on the shores of Silver Lake. The girls kept up with their schoolwork on their own. They played games in the evenings after the chores of the day were finished, and Pa played his fiddle again. He taught Laura and Carrie how to dance the waltz and the polka.

There was even a surprise for Christmas that year. A friend they had met at the railroad camp, Mr. Boast, brought his wife out to Silver Lake to spend the rest of the winter. Mr. and Mrs. Boast arrived on Christmas Eve. They moved into one of the shanties nearby and were delightful company for the Ingallses.

When spring came, the expected rush of settlers began. The townsite of De Smet was laid out nearby, and Pa bought two lots on Main Street. He began building right away, and the family moved into one of his store buildings when the surveyors came back to live in their house.

Then Pa hustled out to the claim site he had found and built a little one-room claim shanty for his family to live in that summer. Life was beginning to look promising again.

Inside the claim shanty

LIFE BY SILVER LAKE

Building the Railroad

*"I wouldn't wonder if you'll live to see a time, Laura, when pretty nearly
everybody'll ride on railroads and there'll hardly be a covered wagon left," said Pa.*

The building of the American railroads began in the 1830's, when Pa and Ma were babies. Nearly forty years later, in 1869, the Union Pacific and Central Pacific lines met, connecting the east and west coasts of the country. A celebration was held when the final spike was driven at Promontory Point in Utah. Now freight, passengers, and mail could travel across the whole country, from New York, Boston or Philadelphia to San Francisco, in about ten days. By horse and wagon this trip took months.

Without the railroad, the Great Plains would not have been settled so quickly. Railroad companies obtained land from the government to build their railroads. About every seven to ten miles along the track, the railroad would lay out a town and sell lots to settlers—farmers and speculators—who wanted to build up the town. The towns were spaced at this distance because trains had to refill their water tanks about every ten miles to keep the steam engines going.

When the Ingallses left the Big Woods by covered wagon for western Minnesota in 1874, they followed the path the railroad took. It led them southwest from Lake City on the Mississippi River to Zumbrota, then west, and finally to the brand-new town of Walnut Grove, where they settled on Plum Creek for a few years. The Walnut Grove depot was built the very same year the Ingallses moved

to Plum Creek, and the railroad continued west seven miles to Tracy, and then turned north.

In 1879, the Chicago and Northwestern Railroad began construction of a line straight west from Tracy toward the southern part of Dakota Territory. When Pa heard from Aunt Docia that more men were needed to help build this railroad, he immediately realized the opportunity the railroad gave for his family to have a new start. He began working for the railroad as bookkeeper and clerk, about seventy miles from Walnut Grove. When the camp was ready to move farther west, Pa sent word, probably by telegraph, to Ma and the girls in Walnut Grove that he would meet them at the end of the line in Tracy and take them by wagon to the new camp at Silver Lake, about forty miles farther west of the old camp.

Ma bought the tickets at the Walnut Grove depot. The agent would have written the starting point and destination on each long, blue cardboard ticket. Passengers paid by the number of miles they were going, about ten cents per mile at the time. Children under the age of twelve, like Carrie and Grace, traveled free. For the three tickets to Tracy from Walnut Grove, Ma would have paid about $2.10—seventy cents for each ticket. She would have paid extra to ship the family's household goods in the freight car.

Laura never forgot her first train ride. She was amazed by the noise, speed, and power of the locomotive that could go as fast as thirty-five miles per hour—about ten times as fast as a horse and wagon! She was charmed by the passenger car, with its large windows and red velvet seats, and she was fascinated by the little tank of drinking water. Some trains on major routes had dining cars at that time, but many people preferred to take their own food along with them or eat in the depots or hotels in the towns where the trains stopped. There was no dining car on the train that Laura rode in 1879. Ma took the girls to a hotel in Tracy to eat dinner that day. It was not until 1902 that dining cars were added to the train that ran through Walnut Grove and Tracy.

Members of the Ingalls family came to rely on the trains after they moved to De Smet. Ma and Pa took Mary to Vinton, Iowa, by train in 1881 to enroll her in the School for the Blind. Mary then learned how to travel by train on her own so that she could return to De Smet for visits. Laura, Almanzo, and Rose traveled by train to Florida in 1891. In 1902, Laura was able to rush back to De Smet by train from her home in Missouri to see Pa before he died. And in 1915, Laura went by train to visit Rose in San Francisco, a journey she described in letters she mailed home to Almanzo. These letters were published after Laura's death in a book called *West From Home*.

Dried-Apple Sauce

Laura gathered up all the paper wrappings, and she helped Ma set on the table
the big platter of golden, fried mush, a plate of hot biscuits, a dish of fried potatoes,
a bowl of codfish gravy and a glass dish full of dried-apple sauce.

Dried-apple sauce was part of the Christmas breakfast that the Ingallses shared with Mr. and Mrs. Boast in the Surveyors' House. Dried apple slices kept longer during the winter than fresh apples; they also took up less room in the pantry. When they had been cooked for a little while, they made an applesauce that tasted as though it had been made from fresh apples.

To make about a quart of applesauce, you will need:

8 ounces dried apple slices	*Sugar*
(available at grocery or	*Ground cinnamon (optional)*
specialty stores)	*Large saucepan*
Boiling water	*Potato masher or food mill*

1. Put the apples in the saucepan and cover with boiling water.
2. Let them soak until they are tender, about 15 minutes. Add more water, if necessary, to keep the apple slices covered.
3. Mash or grind the apples to applesauce consistency. Add sugar to taste.
4. Simmer the applesauce about 3 minutes.
5. Serve the applesauce warm or cold. Sprinkle each serving with a bit of cinnamon if you like. Store any leftover applesauce in the refrigerator.

This recipe serves six.

The Polka and the Waltz

Pa showed them how to hold hands and step to the tune of a polka. Then he played it and they danced while he sang. . . . "Now then," said Pa, "try a bit of a waltz," and the music flowed smoothly in gliding long waves.

When the Ingallses moved into the Surveyors' House for the winter, Pa decided Laura and Carrie were old enough to learn how to dance. The polka and the waltz were two of the most popular dances at the time.

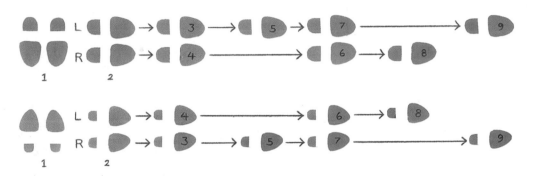

THE POLKA: Polka music is very lively. The rhythm is one-and-two, one-and-two.

1. First the boy puts his right hand lightly on the girl's waist, while her left hand rests on his right shoulder.

2. Then the boy takes the girl's right hand in his left hand, and they turn to face forward. This is called the "promenade position."

3. When the music starts, each takes a step forward with his or her outside foot (the boy's outside foot is his left foot; the girl's outside foot is her right foot).

4. Then each brings his or her inside foot up to the outside foot so that both feet are together.

5. Next each takes another step forward with the outside foot.

6. Now each steps forward, *ahead* of the outside foot, with the inside foot. Do not bring feet together here!

7. Next each brings his or her outside foot up to the inside foot so both feet are together.

8. Then each takes another step forward with the inside foot.

9. Repeat from Step 3. Remember to step *ahead* of the inside foot with the outside foot! Repeat this step-together-step pattern all around the dance floor until the music stops.

THE WALTZ: The rhythm of the waltz is ONE, two, three, ONE, two, three. The partners face each other with the boy's right hand around the girl's waist, her left hand on his right shoulder, and their other hands clasped lightly.

1. The boy takes a big step to the side with his right foot, and the girl takes a big step to the side with her left foot.

2. Next the boy takes a small step to the side with his left foot, and the girl takes a small step to the side with her right foot.

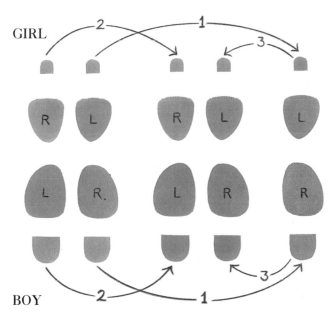

3. Now each takes a small step with the other foot so both feet are together.

4. Repeat this one big step, two small steps pattern over and over again around the dance floor while the music plays. Or you can follow the same step pattern for the polka—just make the steps smoother and more graceful. As Pa said, "Just float on the music, glide smoothly and turn." And remember to dance counterclockwise around the dance floor so you don't run into the other couples!

The Long Winter

"It's going to be a hard winter," Pa said. "The hardest we ever saw."

THE LONG WINTER tells how the Ingalls family managed to survive one of the harshest winters on record in what is now South Dakota. The Ingallses had spent their first summer on their homestead claim, about a mile south of the newly settled town of De Smet. Pa had broken up some of his acres over the summer and planted corn, potatoes, pumpkins, beans, and tomatoes. He also raised hay; he hoped to start a herd of cattle. For the first time, Laura helped Pa with the haying. She was thirteen years old.

As fall progressed on the prairie, Pa noticed the extra-thick walls of the muskrat house in the Big Slough near the claim. He believed it was a sign of a cold winter to come. An unusually early blizzard in October was another sign. The third sign came from an old Indian who passed through town to warn the people of the seven months of blizzards to come. Pa did not waste any more time. He went straight home and told Ma and the girls to start packing for the move into town. They would spend the winter in the store building Pa had built in the spring. The store was much warmer than the shanty and less exposed to the brutal prairie winds. Living in town also meant that buying food and coal would be easier. Like the town's eighty other residents, the Ingallses depended on the trains for regular deliveries of coal, since there were not enough trees on the prairie to provide firewood for fuel.

The Ingallses moved to town just in time. Blizzards came in regularly every few days from November through March. Even worse, there was so much snow that the trains could not get through to the town. The townspeople rationed and stretched what little they had as best they could. The Ingallses' diet consisted of coarse brown bread, potatoes, and turnips. Ma made the flour for the brown bread out of wheat she first had to grind in a coffee mill, one half cup at a time.

Eventually, though, even the wheat began to run out, and people were on the verge of starving. Almanzo Wilder, who lived in town with his brother Royal, had a supply of seed wheat but wanted to plant it in the spring. So when he heard of another farmer with a supply of wheat on his prairie homestead several miles out of town, he offered to go look for it. Almanzo and Cap Garland, a classmate of Laura's, set out on the first clear day. It was a dangerous undertaking. A sudden blizzard could strand them and even kill them. Many times on the cold journey, the horses and sleds fell through the snow across the prairie, and the cold wind nearly froze the young men to death. They found the wheat,

De Smet and the lakes

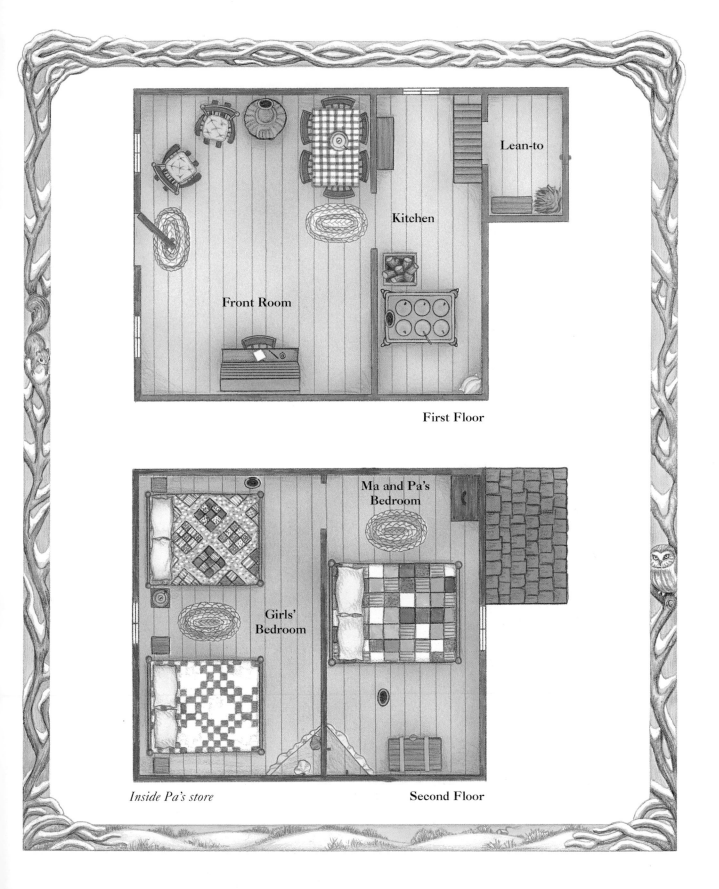

Front Room

Kitchen

Lean-to

First Floor

Ma and Pa's Bedroom

Girls' Bedroom

Inside Pa's store

Second Floor

convinced the farmer to sell them sixty bushels, and got back to town with it just as the next blizzard struck.

The extra wheat Almanzo and Cap brought back kept the people in town from starving. An idea of Pa's kept them from freezing to death. After all the coal in town had been used up, Pa started burning the coarse slough grass for fuel. He twisted a handful of the six-foot-long grass into a "stick" about the size of a piece of firewood. Soon the other families were doing the same thing. The hay burned fast—one stick every five minutes—so the supply had to be replenished constantly. Laura helped Pa twist hay every day for months to keep the stove going.

Each day was the same in that long winter. Ma and the girls took turns grinding wheat, and Pa and Laura twisted hay. The cold made it impossible for school to stay in session or for church services to be held. It was even too cold for Pa to play the fiddle in the evenings.

Finally the blizzards stopped, and in the warm winds of April the frozen prairie began to thaw. By the first week of May, the trains could get through again. The Ingallses celebrated with their friends the Boasts by having Christmas in May. A barrel of Christmas presents and a frozen turkey that the Reverend Alden had sent months before were on one of the first trains to arrive. Ma cooked a turkey dinner with all the trimmings, and Pa played the fiddle once again.

The Mail

"That's not all," Pa went on. "We're going to get the mail, train or no train.
They're sending it through by team, and Gilbert, the mail carrier, is leaving here for Preston
in the morning. He's making a sled now. So if you want to send a letter, you can."

Because there were no telephones on the frontier when Laura was growing up, pioneer families wrote letters to each other to keep in touch with their families and friends who lived miles away. Many of those letters were delivered at least part of the way by the railroads. When the trains bound for De Smet could not get through during the long winter, the mail was delayed. The Ingallses' Christmas packages could not be delivered on time either. Yet even with the trains running regularly, mail sometimes took a long time to be delivered.

Before the trains began to carry the mail, it was delivered by stagecoach or horseback. Sometimes a mail carrier had to walk from one town to another with the mail. This was a slow system. It could take weeks or even months for a letter to get from the east out to California, where people were working in the goldfields. It would even take weeks for a letter to get from Wisconsin to the Kansas prairie!

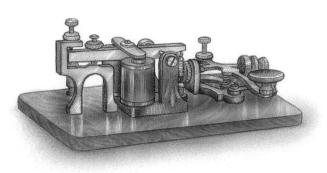

In 1860, the year Ma and Pa married, the Pony Express began carrying mail back and forth from St. Joseph, Missouri, to Sacramento, California. Riders would carry the mail pouches by horseback as fast as the horses could run. They would get a fresh horse about every ten miles and ride about seventy-five miles before passing the mail to another rider. They could cover the distance, some 2,000 miles, in about ten days. At first it cost five dollars to send a half-ounce letter by Pony Express. Several months later, as the service was used more and more, the cost was reduced to a dollar.

The Pony Express system lasted about eighteen months, until telegraph lines stretched across the whole country and could carry messages instantly. Then, eight

years later, when the transcontinental railway was completed, trains began to carry mail from coast to coast. In areas not served by the railroad, however, such as many parts of the Great Plains, delivery by horseback or stagecoach was still common.

When Ma and Pa moved to the Big Woods in 1863, the only way for them to keep in touch with their relatives in Concord, Wisconsin, was by letter. How did a letter from the wilderness of the Big Woods reach eastern Wisconsin?

Whenever Pa went into town, he could take a letter with him to the post office in Pepin to mail back east. Pa would pay three cents to send a half-ounce letter. The postmaster in Pepin would hold the letter until he could send it by boat down to LaCrosse, where it would be put on a train bound for Chicago. The mail bag would be dropped off at the Jefferson Junction station east of Madison, Wisconsin, and the letter would then be given to a mail carrier to take to the post office in Concord. The mail carrier might travel on horseback or on foot. The letter would be held at the post office until it was picked up by the person to whom it was addressed or by a member of that person's family.

There was no post office in Independence, Kansas, when the Ingallses arrived in 1869. Mail was delivered as far as Oswego, about thirty miles east, and had to be picked up by an independent mail carrier, who took it by horseback or by foot to smaller towns around Oswego. L. T. Stephenson was the first to carry mail from Oswego to Independence; he began carrying mail in 1869. Recipients paid him ten cents for every letter he brought from Oswego, and anyone mailing a letter from Independence paid him ten cents to carry it to Oswego. In July of 1870, mail began arriving by stagecoach, and Independence was assigned its first town postmaster, who received an annual salary of $12.

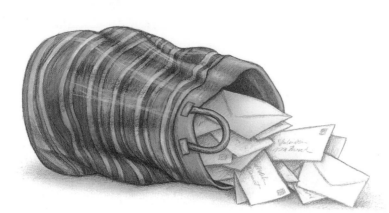

When the Ingalls family lived in De Smet, their mail came to them by train. The train had a separate mail car and a postman who rode in it to sort the mail. He put the mail for each town in its own sack, and when the train reached the town, its sack would be left at the depot. De Smet's postmaster, Mr. Gilbert, would pick up the sack of mail and sort it. He would sort the outgoing mail into eastbound or westbound sacks, and then he would take them to the depot to be put on the trains. Residents would come to the post office and pick up their mail. On the frontier and on the prairie, the post office was most commonly in the corner of a general store or even in the postmaster's home.

Usually all that was necessary for an address was the name of the recipient, the town, and the state. Mail to larger cities needed a street address or post office box. Later, cities were divided into numbered zones. There were no ZIP codes in Laura's day. In fact, they did not come into use until 1963.

In 1885, the year Laura and Almanzo were married, the special delivery system was established. For an extra charge, special delivery mail would be delivered to the recipient personally by a mail carrier rather than being held in the post office, as was customary. In 1896, when Laura, Almanzo, and Rose were living at Rocky Ridge, rural free delivery began. This meant that people who lived on farms now could have their mail delivered to their homes instead of having to go to town to collect it at the post office.

Red-and-White Striped Paper

The table was set and Ma was putting on each plate
a little package wrapped in red-and-white striped paper.

To make them look special, Ma wrapped her Christmas gifts in gift-wrap paper she may have made herself.

To make red-and-white striped paper, you will need:

Newspapers	*Water*
Small disposable dish	*Piece of cotton string, 36" long*
1 jar of red acrylic paint	*Large sheets of plain white paper*

1. Spread newspapers on a flat work surface to protect it.

2. Pour some red paint into the disposable dish; add water to thin it down.

3. Dip the piece of string into the paint to coat it thoroughly.

4. Carefully remove the string from the paint, letting any drips fall back into the dish.

5. Hold each end of the string and lay the string down on the paper. For a wider stripe, roll the string back and forth slightly.

6. Make another stripe about an inch from the first one and continue across the whole width of the paper.

7. Dip the string in the paint again as needed. You can make straight stripes or wavy ones or both.

8. Let the paper dry before wrapping gifts. You can use the paint-soaked string to tie up your package if you like.

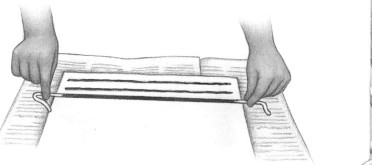

Almanzo's Buckwheat Pancakes

Almanzo had stacked the pancakes with
brown sugar and he had made plenty of them.

Almanzo and his brother Royal often made dozens of pancakes at a time for supper. They would put the stacks of pancakes on a platter and cover them with an extra-large pancake called a "blanket cake" to keep them hot. Then they ate them with molasses or brown sugar, accompanied by slices of sugar-cured and hickory-smoked ham.

To make buckwheat pancakes you will need:

1 cup buckwheat flour	¼ cup oil or melted butter, and
1 cup all-purpose flour	additional oil or butter to
(or whole wheat flour, or	grease the griddle
a combination)	Measuring cup and spoons
2 teaspoons baking powder	2 small bowls
1 teaspoon baking soda	Large bowl
½ teaspoon salt	Mixing spoon
2 eggs, separated	Eggbeater
2 cups buttermilk	Griddle
1 tablespoon molasses	Spatula

1. Beat the egg whites in one small bowl until they are fluffy and form soft peaks.
2. Mix the dry ingredients together in the large bowl.

3. Beat the egg yolks lightly in the second small bowl, and add the buttermilk, molasses, and oil to them.

4. Pour these liquid ingredients into the dry ingredients and stir them together.

5. Stir half of the egg whites into the pancake batter; then gently fold the rest in until it is barely blended.

6. Lightly grease the hot griddle with oil or butter.

7. Spoon the batter onto the griddle in 5" circles.

8. When the pancakes begin to bubble and brown around the edges, turn them over with the spatula and bake the other sides, about a minute, or until done.

9. Serve the pancakes hot with butter and maple syrup, or sprinkle them with brown sugar or molasses as Almanzo did. To keep your pancakes warm, you can cover them with a "blanket cake" or you can put them in a warm oven.

This recipe makes about 12 pancakes.

Little Town on the Prairie

The town was so changed that it seemed like a new place.

Little Town on the Prairie is one of the most carefree of the Little House books. The long winter is over, the town of De Smet is growing, and for the first time, Laura, now fourteen, has a social life.

After the grim days of the long winter had been put behind them, the Ingallses hurried back to their claim. Laura was especially eager, for she preferred the open country on the prairie to life in town.

The family acquired a kitten and a calf, and they made plans to buy a pig and some chickens. Pa had a new plow that made breaking up the prairie sod much quicker and easier. After the garden and crops were planted, Pa built another room onto the little shanty. There were now two small bedrooms as well as a combined living room and kitchen.

De Smet itself was growing fast. Many people were coming in to settle the land, and the town needed new buildings. Pa was a good carpenter, and that summer he helped build many store buildings and the first church in town. While he was working, he learned that a job making shirts was available at Clancy's store, and he asked Laura if she would like it.

At first, Laura did not want to work in town, but she soon changed her mind when she learned she could earn twenty-five cents a day. This money would help add to Mary's college fund, money that the Ingallses had been

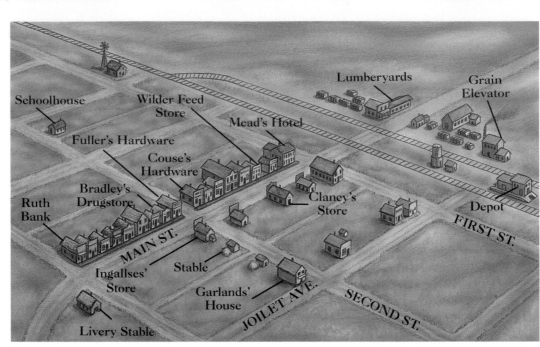

The little town on the prairie

saving for two years. Laura worked six days a week for six weeks and made nine dollars. She gave all the money to Ma and Pa for Mary, and with it, Ma and Pa were finally able to take Mary to college. Ma, Pa, and Mary traveled by train to Vinton, Iowa, and enrolled Mary in the Iowa School for the Blind.

It was lonely at home without Mary, but Laura and Carrie had their own schoolwork to keep them busy. They studied hard and were good students, but this term their teacher was Eliza Jane Wilder, Almanzo's sister, and she seemed to dislike Laura and Carrie from the beginning. To make matters worse, Laura's old enemy from Walnut Grove, Nellie Oleson, was now living in De Smet and coming to school! Nellie and Miss Wilder sometimes made school uncomfortable, but Laura still enjoyed herself with her friends Minnie Johnson, Ida Wright, and Mary Power. There were plenty of fun things to do, including two new fads, autograph albums and name cards.

When Pa moved the family into town again for the winter, Laura began to see that town life could be fun, too. There were birthday parties, "literaries,"

and church meetings to attend with her friends and family. Laura called this time "a whirl of gaiety."

Laura enjoyed herself during these days, but she also wanted to earn a teaching certificate so that she could teach school and help keep Mary in college. Laura spent the next summer and fall studying hard for her certificate and the School Exhibition. She made such a good impression at the Exhibition that she was offered a teaching job!

Laura easily passed the teacher's examination and accepted the job, although she was not quite sixteen. She was to teach school for the next two months, and she would be paid forty dollars, but she would also have to leave home for the first time.

The Town

Now there was always Friday evening to look forward to, and after the second Literary, there was such rivalry between the entertainers that there was news almost every day.

As Laura was growing up, she spent most of her time at home with her family. She was shy and almost fearful of people she did not know well. As a teenager, though, living in the little town of De Smet in Dakota Territory, Laura began to grow more accustomed to socializing with a larger circle of friends and even began to like it.

Prairie towns were very much alike when Laura was a teenager. Towns usually developed around a railroad stop. The railroad companies owned the land along their tracks and plotted out towns where they needed them. Then they sold lots in the towns to people who wanted to start businesses there.

Towns like De Smet were called "T-towns" because they were laid out in the shape of a letter T with the railroad and the depot at the top of the T and a main street running straight down from it. Hotels were usually near the top of the T so that train passengers could find room and board in the town easily. People who wanted to start businesses were quick to buy lots on the main streets of new towns and to build store buildings. Corner lots were particularly valuable, because a building built on a corner could be seen from two directions. Pa bought two corner lots on De Smet's Main Street as soon as they came on the market in 1880.

Community life in prairie towns revolved mostly around the school and the the church. Spelling bees were popular Friday-evening entertainments where children and adults alike competed. Pa won the first spelling bee in De Smet, and Laura was one of the last spellers to sit down that night. Nearly everyone who lived in or near the town would come to the school for the evening, bringing along candles or lanterns to light the way and to light the room for the evening. Literary societies, also held at the school, were popular in prairie

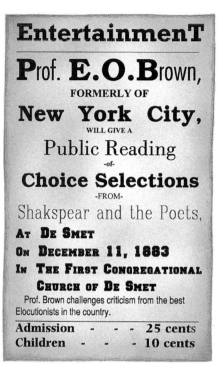

EntertainmenT

Prof. E.O.Brown,

FORMERLY OF

New York City,

WILL GIVE A

Public Reading

-of-

Choice Selections

-FROM-

Shakspear and the Poets,

At De Smet

On December 11, 1883

In The First Congregational
Church of De Smet

Prof. Brown challenges criticism from the best
Elocutionists in the country.

| Admission | - | - | - | 25 cents |
| Children | - | - | - | 10 cents |

towns, too. Citizens would entertain each other with recitations, music, plays, lectures, debates, and other programs.

Churches provided the community with social occasions as well. Church suppers with tables laden with delicious food made by the members were especially popular. The Ingallses were founding members of the churches in both Walnut Grove and De Smet.

As the towns grew, there were more opportunities for socializing. Drugstores, such as Bradley's in De Smet, put in soda fountains and became popular gathering places. Roller rinks, which appeared in the eastern states in 1866, were built in many prairie towns as they became established. De Smet's first roller rink was built in 1884 and became the center of activity for a while. Baseball games were also popular in the summertime.

Many clubs that reflected the interests of the citizens, such as temperance clubs, fraternal organizations, and music clubs, were formed in the early days of

the prairie towns. Members of temperance clubs wanted to keep alcohol out of the town, and fraternal organizations were social clubs that usually helped make improvements in the town.

Theater and musical companies often came to the prairie towns to perform plays and concerts. Speakers would come in to give lectures and orations. Sometimes the programs would be held outside on makeshift stages, but the school or even a church would often be used as an auditorium.

Many prairie towns also had separate auditoriums or "opera houses," and the leaders of De Smet wanted one, too. In 1886, the year after Laura and Almanzo married, Mr. Couse replaced his hardware store at the corner of Main and Second Streets—the first frame building Pa had built in town—with a large two-story brick building, known as the De Smet Opera House. For the next thirty years, entertainments, graduation exercises, traveling shows, speeches, and other events were held there.

Although Laura learned to enjoy the social life of De Smet and, later, of Mansfield, she always preferred the quieter life on the farm. In 1919, she wrote this in an article for *The Missouri Ruralist*:

We who live in the quiet places have the opportunity to become acquainted with ourselves, to think our own thoughts and live our own lives in a way that is not possible for those who are keeping up with the crowd.

Laura's Autograph Book

In Laura's package was a beautiful small book, too. It was thin,
and wider than it was tall. On its red cover, embossed in gold, were the words,

Autograph Album

The pages, of different soft colors, were blank. Carrie had another exactly like it,
except that the cover of hers was blue and gold.

Ma and Pa brought Laura and Carrie autograph books from their trip to Vinton, Iowa, where they had taken Mary to the School for the Blind. Ma said that "autograph albums are all the fashion nowadays," and she thought Laura and Carrie would enjoy them.

To make your own autograph album you will need:

Red construction paper or card stock	Ruler
	Pen
Pastel-colored paper, 2 sheets each of 3 or 4 colors	Hole punch
	Narrow ribbon or cord, about
Scissors	12" long

1. Cut the pastel-colored paper into pieces about 5" wide and 3" long and stack them.

2. Trim the ends so they are even.

3. To make the covers, cut the heavier red paper into two pieces about 5" wide and 3" high.

4. Write "AUTOGRAPH ALBUM" on one piece.

5. On the left side of the cover pages and inside pages, punch a hole about ½" from the top and another hole about ½" from the bottom.

6. Place the stack of inside pages between the cover pages, and run the piece of narrow ribbon or cord through the holes. Tie the ends in a bow on the front of the album.

In Laura's autograph album, her friends wrote verses that they had made up or memorized, and they signed their names to them. Ask your friends to write in your album. You can also make albums for your friends.

IDA WRIGHT'S VERSE TO LAURA:

In memory's golden casket,
Drop one pearl for me.

Your loving friend,
—Ida B. Wright.

MA'S VERSE TO LAURA:

If wisdom's ways you wisely seek,
Five things observe with care,
To whom you speak,
Of whom you speak,
And how, and when, and where.

Your loving mother
—C L Ingalls
De Smet November 15th, 1881

Ma's Thanksgiving Pumpkin Pie

Ma bore in both hands the great pumpkin pie,
baked in her large, square bread-baking tin.

To raise money for the new church, the Ladies' Aid of De Smet planned a New England Supper on Thanksgiving night. Ma made "a mammoth pumpkin pie and the largest milkpan full of baked beans" to take to the supper.

Before Ma could bake the pie, she had to prepare the pumpkin. First she cut it open and scooped out the seeds. Then she peeled off the tough rind. Next she cut the pumpkin into smaller pieces and put them in a pot with some water. She set the pot on the woodstove and kept the fire going until the water boiled; then she simmered the pumpkin until it was very tender. After the pumpkin was cooked, Ma drained it, mashed it, pushed it through a sieve, and drained it some more. *Now* it was ready to make into a pie!

In this recipe we used canned pumpkin since it is easier to cook with, but you can use a fresh pumpkin if you want.

To make pumpkin pie, you will need:

1 unbaked pie crust rolled out to a 12" square	*½ teaspoon ground ginger*
3 eggs	*½ teaspoon ground cloves*
2 cups cooked, mashed pumpkin (1 16-ounce can)	*¼ teaspoon ground nutmeg*
¾ cup brown sugar, firmly packed	*½ teaspoon salt*
1 teaspoon ground cinnamon	*1½ cups milk*
	9" square cake pan
	Medium-size bowl
	Eggbeater or fork

1. Preheat the oven to 425°.

2. Lay the pie crust in the 9" square pan and fit it up around the sides.

3. Flute the edges in a pretty design.

4. Beat the eggs until thoroughly mixed.

5. Add the pumpkin, sugar, and spices and salt, and mix well.

6. Add the milk and mix thoroughly.

7. Pour the pumpkin mixture into the pie crust.

8. Bake the pie at 425° for 15 minutes; then turn the oven down to 350° and continue baking for about 30 minutes more or until a knife put in about an inch from the edge comes out clean. The pie will set a little more as it cools.

9. Cool the pie on a rack before serving. Cut it into squares to serve. Refrigerate any leftover pieces.

Laura's Name Cards

There they were, delicate pink cards, with a spray of pinker roses and blue cornflowers. Her name was printed in thin, clear type: Laura Elizabeth Ingalls.

All of Laura's friends were buying name cards, but Laura was sure she couldn't have any. They were expensive—twenty-five cents a dozen!—but Pa and Ma insisted that Laura buy some. The first person Laura gave one to was Almanzo Wilder.

To make your own name cards, you will need:

Pastel-colored con-truction paper or index cards	*Floral stickers (or colored pictures of flowers)*	*Ruler* *Pencil* *Scissors* *Pen with black ink*

1. With a ruler and pencil, mark off rectangles 2" x 3" on the paper.
2. Cut along the lines.
3. Decorate the left side of the card with your choice of flower pictures or stickers.
4. With the ruler and pencil, very lightly draw a line across the middle of the blank space.
5. On the line, with the black pen, write your name in your best handwriting. (Practice this first on a piece of paper to see how long to make the line.)
6. When the ink is perfectly dry, carefully erase the pencil line.

Make enough cards to give to each of your friends.

These Happy Golden Years

*"Golden years are passing by,
These happy, golden years."*

THESE HAPPY GOLDEN YEARS begins immediately where *Little Town on the Prairie* ends, and it tells of Laura's teaching and courtship years. Laura's first teaching job was at the Brewster school twelve miles south of town. Pa drove Laura across the frozen prairie to the Brewsters' claim shanty, where Laura was to board. Then Pa returned to De Smet, and Laura was living without her family for the first time in her life.

Mr. Brewster had hired Laura to teach the school. He was friendly to Laura, but Mrs. Brewster was sullen and unpleasant. Laura realized that Mrs. Brewster hated living on the prairie, and that was why she was so ill-tempered. Still, her unkindness was hard to live with, and Laura was very homesick. Laura taught five pupils in a flimsy claim shanty on the prairie. She became more and more confident and with Ma's advice even learned how to manage Clarence, the one difficult student in school.

Laura thought those eight weeks of teaching would never end, but with Almanzo Wilder's help she endured them. Every Friday, Almanzo drove to the Brewsters' and took Laura back to De Smet for the weekend. He then drove her back to the Brewsters' on Sunday afternoons. Even on the coldest days, Almanzo made the trip.

Inside the Brewster school

After her two months at the Brewster school were finished, Laura returned to the De Smet school and to her own studies. She taught school twice more over the next year and a half, first at the Perry school near the Ingallses' claim shanty and then at the Wilkins school north of De Smet near Spirit Lake. These teaching experiences were much more pleasant than her two months at the Brewster school.

The money that Laura earned at the Perry school helped buy a small parlor organ as a surprise for Mary when she came home from college. Pa built another room onto the little claim shanty for the organ. Ma said they must not call it a claim shanty anymore—it had become a real house.

The rides with Almanzo had not stopped when Laura returned from the Brewsters'. During the winter, Almanzo took Laura on sleigh rides, and when spring came they went on buggy rides. They rode over the prairie, picked wild grapes, and filled the buggy with the wild roses that bloomed everywhere in the spring. Laura even helped Almanzo break a frisky pair of colts, Barnum and Skip. It was on one of their drives with the colts that Almanzo gave Laura a beautiful garnet and pearl engagement ring. When he told her he could build her only a little house, Laura replied that she had always lived in little houses and that she liked them.

Over the next months, in between going to school and teaching, Laura began working on her trousseau, with Ma's help. Laura needed new clothes and sheets, pillowcases, towels, and quilts for setting up her own household. Ma had always stitched these items by hand. One day, though, Pa brought home a new sewing machine he had bought in town. The wonderful new machine made the sewing go so much faster!

Almanzo and Laura were married at the Reverend Brown's house near the Ingallses' farm. It was a simple ceremony, because they could not afford a large or elaborate wedding. They went back to Ma and Pa's house for a wedding dinner and then drove away to the new house Almanzo had built. Laura called it their "little gray home in the west."

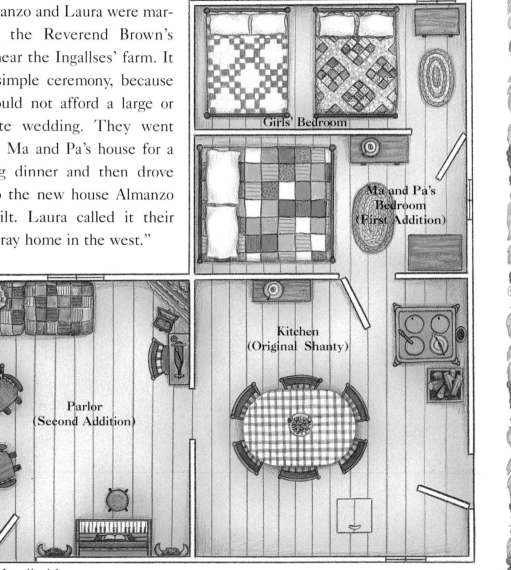

Girls' Bedroom

Ma and Pa's Bedroom (First Addition)

Kitchen (Original Shanty)

Parlor (Second Addition)

Inside the Ingallses' house

Prairie Schools

*A small window by the door let in a block of sunshine. Beyond it, in the
corner by the stove, stood a small table and a chair. "That is the teacher's table,"
Laura thought, and then, "Oh my; I am the teacher."*

Most of the schools in rural America at the time Laura was growing up were
one-room schoolhouses. There were students of all ages and all grades in one
room, with one teacher for everyone. The number of students depended on the
size of the district. In Laura's first teaching job, she had five students. She had
only two students in the Perry school! Some teachers reported having up to

sixty students enrolled in one school. By the time Laura finished her teaching career in 1885, there were about fifty schools, most of them one-room schoolhouses, in the county.

Children usually began school when they were six years old and could continue until they were sixteen. Laura began school in the Big Woods when she was four years old. There were eight "grades," but students had to master one level before moving up to the next. Once they finished public school, they could go to a private school or university for more advanced education if they could afford it.

Attendance was not required when Laura was growing up, and many students on the frontier could not attend school regularly. If children were needed on their parents' farms to help with planting or harvesting or other work, they did not go to school. They sometimes studied at home to make up for what they missed at school.

School could be held in any season, depending on the wishes of the district. Some schools did not have winter terms because heating the school would have cost too much. Some fall terms did not start until mid-October so that children could help with the harvesting on their farms. Some districts had summer school terms.

A typical school day when Laura was growing up, regardless of the season, started at eight or nine o'clock in the morning and lasted until mid-afternoon. There would be a break for lunch and short recesses in the morning and afternoon.

Students had to bring their own schoolbooks to school. The *McGuffey's Eclectic Readers* were the most popular schoolbooks of the mid-1800's. They were first published in 1836 by William Holmes McGuffey, a schoolteacher in Ohio. They contained lessons on spelling, pronunciation, grammar, history, and geography interspersed with poems and famous literary passages. Students could buy their schoolbooks at the town's general store. However, many students often used the same books their parents had used in their school days. Ma gave Mary and Laura her schoolbooks for their studies—a speller, an arithmetic book, and a reader.

In addition to their own schoolbooks, students had to provide their own school supplies. Slates and slate pencils, pencils and paper, and pens and ink could be bought at the general store for a few cents each. Students took their own lunches to school, too, usually in small tin pails. Lunch pails were left with the coats at the back of the schoolroom until noon.

The teacher's desk was at the front of the room, sometimes on a raised platform. A blackboard, usually just wooden boards painted black, was on the wall behind the teacher's desk. The teacher wrote lessons on the blackboard with chalk for the students to copy onto their slates or papers. Sometimes the students practiced their arithmetic or writing on the blackboard.

The teacher was not only responsible for teaching the students their lessons and maintaining good order, but also had to keep the classroom clean and keep the stove going in the winter to heat the room. Teachers were paid about five or six dollars a week, depending on how much the school district could afford. Teachers often lived with their students' families as partial payment for teaching.

Male teachers were paid more than female teachers. In addition, female teachers in many frontier communities were expected to follow certain rules of behavior. They could not marry or even "keep company" with men. They were supposed to stay at home at night except to attend a church or school program. They could not dye their hair or dress in bright colors, and they were required to wear at least two petticoats! Nonetheless, many young women were eager to become teachers, because teaching was one of the few professions available to them at that time. Laura, her mother, and her mother's mother were all school-teachers before they married.

Mary's Beaded Bracelet and Ring

Laura's gift was a bracelet of blue and white beads strung on thread and woven together, and Carrie's was a ring of pink and white beads interwoven.

The first time Mary came home for a visit from the school for the blind, she brought gifts she had made from tiny beads—a lamp mat for Ma, a doll's chair for Grace, a bracelet for Laura, and a ring for Carrie.

To make a beaded bracelet or ring you will need:

At least two colors of small beads (available at craft stores)
Heavy-duty thread

Needle
Bracelet fastener (available at craft stores)

1. Measure your wrist or finger. Cut 3 pieces of thread, each about 12" longer than the measurement.

2. Thread a needle with one piece of thread and tie a bead onto the thread about 5" from the end.

3. Slip beads one at a time over the needle, alternating colors.

4. String enough beads on the thread to go around your wrist or finger, plus about ½" extra.

5. Tie the last bead onto the thread. There should be about 5" of thread left on either end of the beaded string.

6. Carefully remove the needle. Set the string aside.

7. Make two more strings of beads the same way. Fasten the three strings together by tying all the right ends to each other.

8. Loosely braid the beaded strings, and check to see if the bracelet or ring will fit. (If necessary, braid the strings more tightly, or add or remove some beads, to make it fit.)

9. Tie the thread ends together.

10. If you are making a bracelet, tie one half of the bracelet fastener on each end of the combined beaded strings, right next to the beads. Clip off extra thread.

11. If you are making a ring, fit the braided bead strings to your finger, have someone tie the end threads in a secure knot, and cut off the extra. The ring is ready to slip on your finger.

Popcorn Balls

When Laura's kettle was full of popped corn,
Ma dipped some into a large pan, poured a thin trickle of the boiling molasses over it,
and then buttering her hands, she deftly squeezed handfuls of it into popcorn balls. Laura
kept popping corn and Ma made it into balls until the large dishpan
was heaped with their sweet crispness.

On Christmas Eve it began to snow, and Pa was afraid it would "turn into a blizzard." So instead of going to the church service in town, the Ingallses decided to celebrate Christmas Eve at home. They made popcorn balls, tied Christmas candy in pink mosquito netting bundles, and sang their favorite songs while Pa played the fiddle.

To make popcorn balls you will need:

4 quarts popped corn	*Measuring cup and spoons*
½ cup molasses	*Large bowl*
2 cups brown sugar	*Large saucepan*
4 tablespoons butter	*Candy thermometer or cup of*
⅓ cup water	*cold water*
Butter for your hands	*Mixing spoon*
	Waxed paper

1. Pour the popcorn into a large bowl that leaves plenty of room for mixing.
2. Combine the molasses, brown sugar, butter, and water in the saucepan.
3. Bring this mixture to a boil, and keep it boiling over low to medium heat until it reaches 250° on the candy thermometer or until a few drops of it form a hard ball in cold water. This will take about 20 minutes.
4. Carefully pour the hot syrup over the popped corn, and mix it with a spoon. Set aside to cool at least 10 or 15 minutes.

5. Butter your hands well. When the popped corn mixture is cool enough to handle but still warm enough for the syrup to remain liquid, gather handfuls and press them lightly into balls about the size of tennis balls or baseballs. *Be very careful not to burn yourself! The molasses mixture can be extremely hot.*

6. Work quickly to keep from burning your hands, and keep buttering your hands to keep them from sticking to the popcorn balls.

7. Set the popcorn balls on waxed paper to harden.

Pile the popcorn balls in a big dish to enjoy right away, or wrap them in waxed paper or plastic wrap to keep for a day or two.

CHAPTER

Ten

The First Four Years

It would be a fight to win out in this business of farming, but strangely she felt her spirit rising for the struggle.

PUBLISHED IN 1971, after Laura, Almanzo, and their daughter, Rose, had died, *The First Four Years* tells the story of Laura and Almanzo's first four years of marriage and their struggle to make a living on the Dakota prairie. Laura had written the first draft of this manuscript after finishing the eight other Little House books, but she had not rewritten or revised it. The original title of the manuscript was *The First Three Years and a Year of Grace.*

After Laura died, the handwritten manuscript remained in Rose's possession. Rose then gave the manuscript to her heir, Roger Lea MacBride, for safekeeping. After Rose died in 1968, Mr. MacBride had the original draft published, because so many people wanted to know what had happened to Laura and Almanzo after their wedding. *The First Four Years* is the last of the books by Laura Ingalls Wilder, and, like the other eight, it stands as a testament to Laura's strength and courage on the frontier.

After their wedding dinner, Laura and Almanzo drove to the small house Almanzo had built for them on his tree claim north of town. Laura saw it now for the first time, and called it "a bright and shining little house." There was a sitting room, a bedroom, a pantry with beautiful cabinets and drawers, all made by Almanzo, and a lean-to in which Almanzo had set up the cookstove. The

Laura and Almanzo's first house

house was surrounded by thousands of little trees—mostly cottonwoods, willows, and box elders—which Almanzo had planted as part of his bargain with the government: to plant ten acres of trees on the land in exchange for ownership of the land.

Although Laura had always helped Ma at home, she still had much to learn about running a household on her own. Cooking an entire meal herself was harder than she thought, and she made a few mistakes at first. Soon, though, Laura became as expert as Ma in the kitchen.

Almanzo and Laura worked together on the tree claim and on Almanzo's homestead claim about a mile away. They planted their oats and wheat with high hopes for a good harvest, but drought, hailstorms, blizzards, and fire dashed many of their dreams. They sank more and more into debt. They rented the tree claim to another farmer and moved to the homestead. Then they sold the homestead and moved back to the tree claim, all to lessen their debts.

While they were living in the homestead house, their daughter, Rose, was born. They named her for the beautiful wild roses that covered the prairie every spring.

When Rose was one year old, Laura and Almanzo became gravely ill with diphtheria. They eventually recovered, but Almanzo tried to do too much heavy work on the farm before he was strong enough. He was struck with partial paralysis that weakened his legs so much that for a while he could hardly walk. Even though he regained some of his strength, he walked with a limp the rest of his life.

There were still more tragedies the young couple had to endure. Their second child, a boy, lived only a few weeks. Soon after he died, a fire in the kitchen stove went out of control. Laura snatched Rose up and ran from the house. Neighbors hurried to help put out the fire, but in the hot summer wind, the flames quickly burned the house and nearly everything in it. Only Laura's silverware, which was her wedding present from Almanzo, their deed box, some old clothes, and a few of the glass dishes from their first Christmas were saved.

Laura did not know how they could go on, but Almanzo reminded her that they still had their livestock in the barn. He quickly built another little house for them to live in that winter, and they began all over again. In spite of all their hardships, their debts, and their losses, they were determined to keep on farming.

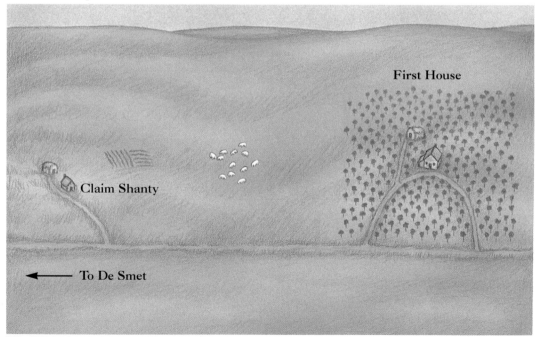

The Wilders' tree claim and homestead

Medicine

Mrs. Power was a friendly, jolly Irish woman.
The first Laura knew of her being there was hearing her say, "Sure she'll
be all right, for it's young she is. Nineteen you say, the very age of my Mary.
But we'd better have the doctor out now, I'm thinking."

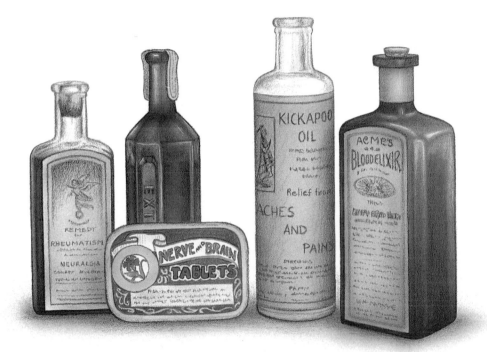

When Laura gave birth to her daughter, Rose, she was attended by both a midwife, Mrs. Power, and a doctor. Since Laura lived close to town, the doctor was able to come quickly when he was needed. But on the frontier, a doctor was often hours away.

If a doctor was needed in an emergency on the prairie, he could be sent for. To find him, someone would walk or ride a horse to locate the doctor and bring him back. When the telegraph and railroads were built, the doctor could be notified by telegraph and take the train to his patient. All these methods, though, took time, and many times patients grew worse or even died before the doctor arrived.

When the Ingallses lived in Kansas, they were fortunate to have a doctor living nearby to treat them when they were sick with "fever 'n' ague." Dr. George Tann had come to Indian Territory from Pennsylvania about the same time as the Ingallses and lived about two miles west of the Ingalls homestead. Dr. Tann gave the Ingallses a bitter medicine called quinine to relieve the symptoms—high fever and chills—caused by malaria. Like most doctors of the time, he was not formally trained as a physician, since at that time, doctors did not have to be certified or licensed to practice medicine. But Dr. Tann had learned how to treat many maladies, probably by working with another doctor.

Mint

When the Ingallses moved to Walnut Grove, the nearest doctor lived in New Ulm, about thirty-five miles to the east. Pa had to send for him when Ma was sick in 1876, and again in 1879 when Mary was stricken with the high fever that eventually led to her blindness.

When women had babies, they usually called on the women who lived nearby to help them. Some of the women who were more experienced in delivering babies were called midwives although, like doctors, they

Dandelion

had no formal training. A neighbor, Mrs. Scott, helped Ma deliver Carrie in Kansas in August of 1870. By the time Laura gave birth to Rose in 1886, however, there was a doctor in De Smet who came to help with the delivery.

Because doctors were scarce and often far away, most families relied on home remedies for their ailments. The recipes for these remedies were handed down through families for many generations. Like most pioneer women, Ma would have had her own recipes for tonics and curatives. Many of the ingredients, such as wild herbs, tree roots, and barks, could be found in the woods. Pioneer women planted others, such as mint, rhubarb, and dandelion, in their gardens.

Mustard

For colds and fever, pioneer women generally made sassafras tea; they steeped the root from the sassafras plant in hot water to make a strong, spicy brew. They ground up mustard seed and mixed it with flour and water to make into a poultice to ease the discomfort of a chest cold or sore muscles. Willow leaves and bark could be made into teas that would ease pain and fever, much as we use aspirin or acetaminophen today. Thyme and horehound were used to relieve coughs. Onions and garlic were believed to prevent infections and to relieve high blood pressure, and milkweed sap was thought to help warts, poison ivy, and other skin problems.

The latter half of the nineteenth century was the era of the "patent medicine," so called because their formulas were said to be patented with the government, thus giving customers the impression that the medicines would work. Knowing how desperate the pioneers could be for treatment of diseases, entrepreneurs bottled concoctions they claimed would cure everything from indigestion to typhoid. Despite their extravagant claims, though, these "medicines" were hardly more than flavored whiskey.

Around the turn of the century, the government began to require physicians to have more formal training and certification, and preparations claiming to cure diseases began to be regulated. Home remedies continued to be popular, though. Here is a recipe from one of Almanzo's notebooks:

HEALING OINTMENT

Mutton tallow	*1 lb.*
Oreganum Oil	*1 oz.*
Camphor gum	*1 oz.*
Tinc. of iodine	*1 oz.*
Venus turpentine	*1 oz.*
Balsam of fir or oil	*1 oz.*
Gum powder oil	*1 oz.*
Alum powder	*1 oz.*

Good for wounds in man or beast.

Geraniums in Decorated Tin Cans

*She would have some geraniums growing in cans on the
windows soon and then it would be simply beautiful.*

The tin cans from the general stores of Laura's day were very fancy and made fine flowerpots. Geraniums were placed on windowsills not just because they were colorful but also because they helped keep flies and other insects away.

To make decorated tin cans for geraniums you will need:

1 geranium plant in a pot　　　　　*Permanent markers or acrylic*
1 tin can a little larger and　　　　　　*paint*
*　　taller than the pot, with all*　　*Gravel*
*　　labels removed*

1. Using permanent markers or acrylic paint, draw designs on the tin can. Or paste a pretty piece of fabric around the can, or glue small beads or shells on it.

2. When the can is dry, put a layer of gravel about an inch deep in the tin can.

3. Set the geranium plant, in its pot, in the can so it rests on top of the gravel.

4. Place in a sunny spot. Water the geranium just often enough to keep the soil damp, but not soaking wet. Pick off the blossoms as they die. The geranium should bloom all summer, maybe longer!

You can sometimes find replicas of old-fashioned tin cans in many craft stores and use them for flowerpots, too.

Hailstone Ice Cream

"And now let's make some ice cream," Manly said. "You stir it up,
Laura, and I'll gather up hailstones for ice to freeze it."

It was midsummer, nearly time for Laura and Almanzo (whom Laura called Manly) to harvest their first crop of wheat, when a hailstorm struck. Some of the stones were "as large as hen's eggs." The storm ruined the wheat. "There is no great loss without some small gain," as Ma used to say, so Manly suggested using the hailstones to make ice cream, a rarity on the hot Dakota plains.

Here is a recipe for homemade ice cream that you can make anytime, whether or not there is a hailstorm.

To make hailstone ice cream, you will need:

1 quart heavy cream
¾ cup sugar
1 teaspoon vanilla
Ice cubes (a gallon or more)
Rock salt
Mixing bowl

Eggbeater or whisk
Large coffee can (or jar) with a
*   lid*
Large pan or bowl, at least 6"
*   larger in diameter than the*
*   coffee can or jar*

1. Whip the heavy cream until soft peaks form.
2. Add sugar and vanilla.
3. Pour the mixture into the large coffee can or jar. There should be about 2" or 3" of air space at the top to allow for expansion in freezing.
4. Put the lid on the jar and make sure it is tightly closed.
5. Set the container into the larger pan, and pour ice cubes around it about halfway up; sprinkle a layer of rock salt on top of the ice. Add more ice to within

about an inch of the top of the container, and add more salt.

6. Twist the inner container back and forth, keeping the mixture moving while it freezes. You can rest for a few minutes at a time, then twist some more. Pour off the water as the ice melts, and add more ice to keep it high.

7. Check the mixture after about half an hour to see if it is thick enough to be ice cream; when it is about the consistency of "soft-serve" ice cream, you can spoon it into dishes to serve. Or you can freeze it awhile longer to make it harder.

This recipe makes 8 servings.

There was no such thing as an ice-cream cone in 1886, the year of Laura and Almanzo's hailstorm. Cones for ice cream were not invented until 1904, during the St. Louis World's Fair, so Laura and Almanzo would have served their ice cream in dishes (perhaps the same ones they had ordered from Montgomery Ward for Christmas) and eaten it with a spoon.

The Rocky Ridge Years

There is everything here already that one could want.

On the Way Home

THE FIRST FOUR YEARS ends when Laura is twenty-two years old, and Laura did not write any more books about her life with Almanzo and Rose. Her story does not end with the Little House books, though. After the first four years of their married life together, years that were marked by heartache and hardship, Laura and Almanzo left South Dakota. They tried living in Florida in hopes that the warmer climate would help Almanzo's health, but Laura did not like the heat. They returned to De Smet temporarily, but continued to look for another place to make a fresh start. They heard that Missouri, "the Land of the Big Red Apple," was supposed to have good farming land, and that the climate was temperate enough to suit both Laura and Almanzo. They worked and saved and finally had enough money to buy a farm. So in 1894, they said good-bye to Ma and Pa, Mary, Carrie, and Grace, and all their friends in De Smet. They packed their things in a little wagon, hitched up the horse, and headed south. Although Laura did not write a book about this journey, she did keep a journal during the trip that was published after her death. It is called *On the Way Home*.

After about six weeks of traveling, Laura and Almanzo found just the place they were looking for. The town was Mansfield, about fifty miles east of

The way to Rocky Ridge

Springfield, and the farm they wanted was only a mile from town. It had apple trees, a little stream, and lots of trees and rocks. In fact, it had so many rocks that Laura named their new farm Rocky Ridge.

The Wilders started out living in the one-room log cabin that was already on

Inside the log cabin

the forty-acre property. Almanzo soon added a lean-to kitchen to the cabin.

Then, after clearing the land and planting a large apple orchard, the Wilders set about making Rocky Ridge a real farm. They built barns for livestock and began work on a farmhouse near the log cabin. The cabin's lean-to kitchen was moved over to the new site and became the kitchen of the new house. They built additions onto the new house and added more land over the next twenty years as they could afford to.

Laura and Almanzo worked very hard to make the farm successful. Laura raised chickens, and Almanzo bred Morgan horses. They also kept cows and goats. As the farm became more established, Laura became involved with other projects as well. In 1911, she began to write articles for *The Missouri Ruralist*, a weekly journal for farmers. She was also secretary-treasurer of the Mansfield Farm Loan Association and was active in some of the women's clubs in Mansfield. She became famous for her gingerbread and made it for many community suppers and picnics. Even though she was busy with the farm, her article writing, and community activities, Laura still had time to write poems. Here is a poem Laura wrote about spring at Rocky Ridge.

The wild woods things are calling,
And the heart in answer thrills,
For it's springtime in the Ozarks,
It is bloom time in the Hills.

The dogwood blooms along the "draws,"
The redbud's all aglow.
The pears and plums and cherries
Look like wreaths of drifted snow.

The buttercups and violets
Have blossomed in the night,
The peach trees are all showing pink
And the apple trees are white.

Rock House

Ravine

Log Cabin

Barn

Farmhouse

Henhouse

To Mansfield

Rocky Ridge Farm

When Rose had grown up and become an accomplished writer and journalist, she encouraged her mother to write down her childhood frontier experiences to share with other people. So over a span of twelve years, beginning in 1930, Laura wrote the Little House books. Since their publication, these books have sold millions of copies. They have been translated into dozens of languages and are read all over the world.

Laura received hundreds of fan letters from children who wanted to tell her how much they loved her books. For many years, Laura answered each letter herself, by hand. She would write notes on the backs of the envelopes to remind herself what questions the children had asked, so that she could answer all their questions in her letters. When Laura got older, and was receiving too much fan mail to answer each letter individually, she composed a form letter that answered the most frequently asked questions about herself, her family, and the people mentioned in the books. Here is the letter:

Dear Children:

I was born in the "Little House in the Big Woods" of Wisconsin on February 7 in the year 1867. I lived everything that happened in my books. It was a long story, filled with sunshine and shadow, that we have lived since "These Happy Golden Years.". . .

After our marriage Almanzo and I lived for a little while in the little gray house on the tree claim. In the year 1894 we and our little daughter Rose left Dakota in a covered wagon and moved to a farm in the Ozarks. We cleared the land and built our own farm house. Eventually we had 200 acres of improved land, a herd of cows, good hogs, and the best laying flock of hens in the country. For many years we did all our own work, but now almost all of the land has been rented or sold. For recreation we used to ride horseback or in our buggy—later on, our Chrysler. We read and played music and attended church socials.

In 1949 Almanzo died at the age of 92. We had been married 63 years. Our daughter, Rose Wilder Lane, the novelist, now lives in Connecticut.

You may be interested to know what happened to some of the other people you met in my books. Ma and Pa lived for a while on their homestead and then moved into town where Pa did carpentry. After Mary graduated from the College for the Blind she lived at home. She was always cheerful and busy with her work, her books and music. Carrie worked for The De Smet News for a while after finishing high school, and then she married a mine owner and moved to the Black Hills. Grace married a farmer and lived a few miles outside of De Smet. All of them have been dead for some years now.

Mary Power married the young banker and did not live many years. Ida married her Elmer and moved to California. Cap Garland was killed in the explosion of a threshing machine engine. Nellie Oleson went East, married, and moved to Louisiana where she is now buried.

Several years before Almanzo's death he and I took a trip back to De Smet for a reunion with our old friends. Many of the old buildings had been replaced. Everywhere we went we recognized faces, but we were always surprised to find them old and gray like ourselves, instead of being young as in our memories. There is one thing that will always remain the same to remind people of little Laura's days on the prairie, and that is Pa's fiddle*, which is now in Memorial Hall of the State Historical Society at Pierre, South Dakota. Every year at a public concert, someone plays on it the songs Pa used to play.

The "Little House" Books are stories of long ago. Today our way of living and our schools are much different; so many things have made living and learning easier. But the real things haven't changed. It is still best to be honest and truthful; to make the most of what we have; to be happy with simple pleasures and to be cheerful and have courage when things go wrong. Great improvements in living have been made because every American has always been free to pursue his happiness, and so long as Americans are free they will continue to make our country ever more wonderful.

With love to you all and best wishes for your happiness, I am

Sincerely, your friend,

Laura Ingalls Wilder

* Now in the Laura Ingalls Wilder–Rose Wilder Lane Home Association Mansfield, Missouri.

—128—

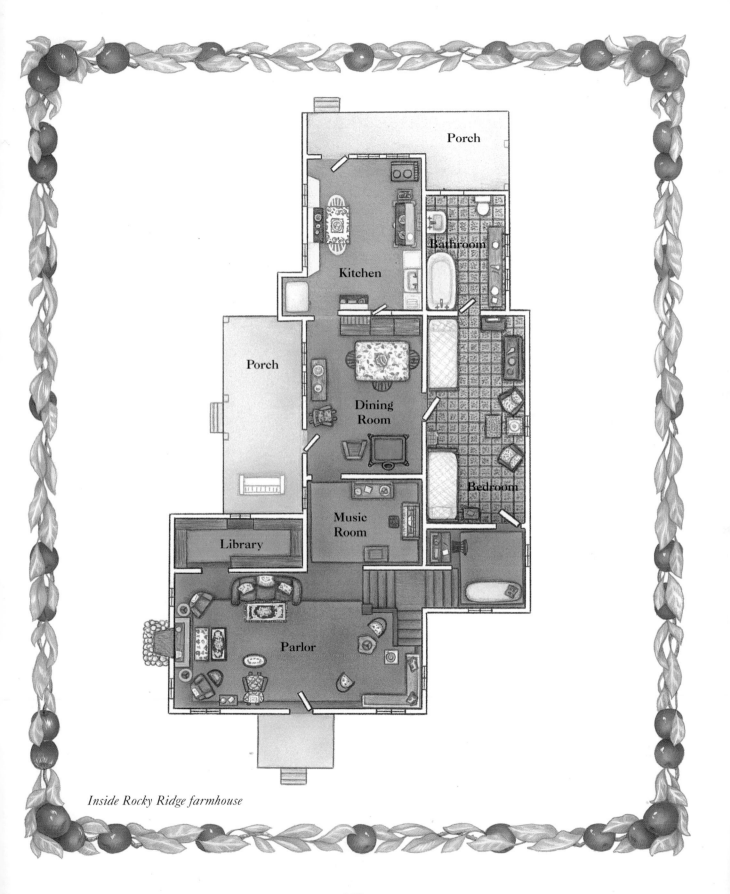

Porch

Kitchen

Bathroom

Porch

Dining
Room

Bedroom

Music
Room

Library

Parlor

Inside Rocky Ridge farmhouse

Almanzo died at Rocky Ridge Farm in 1949. Laura died eight years later, three days after her ninetieth birthday. Their daughter, Rose, died in 1968 at her home in Danbury, Connecticut. All are buried in the Mansfield cemetery, only a few miles from Rocky Ridge Farm.

Although Laura lived over sixty years on Rocky Ridge Farm, she never forgot her childhood homes on the prairie. As an adult, she recorded her enduring connection to the prairie landscape in this poem:

You ask me to sing you a song of the plains,
Of the wide treeless wastes where the free winds blow.
Shall I tell of their beauties when green in the spring,
Or sing of their terrors when swept by the snow?

Shall I tell of their cold, their heat and their storms,
Of their warm, bright days and their dusty weather,
Of how they are loved and hated at once,
For their kindness and cruelty blended together?

Oh, yes, I will sing you a song of the plains
I love them and hate them and fear them, but still,
I will sing to you of their beauty and charm
While I rest safe in the lee of a hill.

Laura's Gingerbread

Laura's gingerbread was a favorite in the Mansfield community, and Laura was often asked to share her recipe for it. Here is her recipe, modified for a modern kitchen.

To make Laura's gingerbread, you will need:

Measuring spoons

9" x 9" baking pan

Small bowl

Mixing spoon

2-cup measuring cup

Large bowl

Cake tester (or fork)

1 cup brown sugar

½ cup shortening

1 cup molasses

2 teaspoons baking soda

1 cup boiling water

3 cups all purpose flour

1 teaspoon each ginger, cinna-

mon, allspice, nutmeg, and

cloves

½ teaspoon salt

Shortening to grease baking pan

1. Preheat oven to 350°. Grease a 9" x 9" baking pan.

2. Blend the sugar and shortening in the small bowl. Mix in the molasses.

3. Measure out a cup of boiling water in the 2-cup measuring cup. *Be careful— the water is hot!* Add the baking soda and mix well.

4. In the large bowl, sift together the flour and the spices. Add all other ingredients, mix well, and pour into prepared pan.

5. Bake for 45 minutes or until cake tester or fork comes out clean.

6. Serve this warm or at room temperature. It is delicious with applesauce or whipped cream that has been whipped to soft peaks and sweetened just a little. Laura herself liked to add chocolate frosting! She wrote in her recipe, "Chocolate frosting adds to the goodness."

Laura Ingalls Wilder, at age 70

CHAPTER Twelve

Laura and Little House Through the Years

LAURA GREW UP in the late 1800's and lived well into the twentieth century. Her life spanned some of the most exciting and interesting times in America. During her childhood, the edges of the frontier were being pushed farther and farther west by immigrants and by families like the Ingallses, who came from the east looking for land and new opportunities. States were rapidly forming and joining the nation. Many things that we use and take for granted today, such as the elevator and the automobile, were invented. Writers like Mark Twain and Louisa May Alcott were publishing their classic books as Laura grew up. Laura also lived through some of the nation's most turbulent and devastating times, including Reconstruction after the Civil War and, in the twentieth century, the Great Depression and the two world wars.

In this time line, we have highlighted some significant historical and cultural events that occurred during Laura's lifetime. It obviously could not include every event, so it concentrates on events that are mentioned in the Little House books or may have made a difference to Laura and her family's lives. The events that are in red describe significant moments in the lives of the Ingalls and Wilder families.

The 1860's

1860
❖Charles Phillip Ingalls and Caroline Lake Quiner are married in Concord, Wisconsin, on February 1.

❖Abraham Lincoln is elected president of the United States.

1861
❖Eliza Quiner marries Peter Ingalls.

❖The Civil War begins at Fort Sumter, South Carolina.

❖The Dakota Territory is formed.

1862
❖Joseph Quiner is killed at the Battle of Shiloh.

❖Congress passes the Homestead Act, which gives 160 acres of land to any U.S. citizen who lives on it.

1863
❖The Ingallses move to the Big Woods.

❖In September, Charles and Caroline buy eighty acres for $335 with Uncle Henry and Aunt Polly Quiner.

❖The Emancipation Proclamation, freeing all slaves, goes into effect.

❖Lincoln delivers his Gettysburg Address.

❖Lincoln proclaims the last Thursday in November as a national Day of Thanksgiving.

1865
❖Mary Amelia Ingalls is born on January 10, in Pepin, Wisconsin.

❖Two of Pa's brothers, Hiram and James, join the Minnesota Volunteers and fight in the Civil War.

❖General Robert E. Lee surrenders to General Ulysses S. Grant at Appomattox.

❖Abraham Lincoln is assassinated on April 14 by John Wilkes Booth.

❖Congress passes the 13th Amendment, abolishing slavery.

1866
❖Almanzo, age 9, wins the blue ribbon for his giant pumpkin at the Franklin, New York, county fair.

❖Alfred Nobel invents dynamite.

1867
❖Laura Elizabeth Ingalls is born on February 7, in Pepin, Wisconsin.

❖Almanzo Wilder is ten years old.

1868
❖The Ingalls family moves to Chariton County, Missouri.

❖The Osage Indians sign a treaty with the United States government for their land in Kansas Reserve.

❖Louisa May Alcott's *Little Women* is published.

❖Congress passes the 14th Amendment, granting citizenship to African Americans.

1869
❖The Ingalls family leaves Chariton County, Missouri, and settles in Montgomery County, Kansas.

❖The first railroad linking the east and west coasts of the entire United States is completed.

❖The first postcards are issued.

The 1870's

1870
✤Laura is three years old.

✤Caroline Celestia (Carrie) Ingalls is born on August 3 in Montgomery County, Kansas.

✤Congress passes the 15th Amendment, granting the right to vote regardless of race, color, or previous condition of servitude.

1871
✤The Ingalls family moves back to Pepin, Wisconsin.

✤Laura attends school for the first time.

✤*The Wonders of the Animal World* (Pa's "Big Green Animal Book") by G. Hartwig is published.

✤Montgomery Ward opens the first catalogue house.

✤P. T. Barnum opens his circus, "The Greatest Show on Earth," in New York.

1873
✤Congress passes the Timber Culture Act, granting 160 acres of timberland to any U.S. citizen who cares for 40 acres for five years.

1874
✤The Ingalls family moves to Walnut Grove, Minnesota.

✤Tom Quiner, Ma's brother, joins the first party of prospectors in the Black Hills of western South Dakota.

✤The first American zoo is established in Philadelphia.

✤The ice cream soda makes its debut at the Franklin Institute in Philadelphia.

1875
✤Charles Frederic (Freddie) Ingalls is born in Walnut Grove on November 1.

✤The Wilder family moves from Malone, New York, to Spring Valley, Minnesota; Almanzo is eighteen years old.

1876
✤Baby Freddie Ingalls dies on August 27.

✤The Ingalls family moves to Burr Oak, Iowa, to help run the Burr Oak House.

1877
✤Grace Pearl Ingalls is born on May 23, in Burr Oak, Iowa.

✤The Ingalls family returns to Walnut Grove, Minnesota.

✤Thomas Edison invents the phonograph.

✤The first U.S. patent for the telephone is granted to Alexander Graham Bell.

✤The Sioux Indians, led by chiefs Sitting Bull and Crazy Horse, defeat General Custer and the Seventh Cavalry in the Battle of Little Bighorn.

✤Grasshoppers are declared "Public Enemy #1" in Minnesota, and the government offers children up to fifty cents for every bushel of dead grasshoppers collected.

1878
✤Laura wins a reference Bible for reciting 104 Golden Texts and Central Truths perfectly.

✤W. A. Burpee begins selling seeds by catalogue.

1879
✤Mary falls ill and slowly loses her sight.

✤The Ingalls family moves to the Dakota Territory and helps settle the town of De Smet.

✤Almanzo, his brother Royal, and their sister Eliza Jane file homestead claims for land near De Smet.

1880

✤Laura is thirteen years old.

✤The Ingallses move into their new homestead, but return to town after an early blizzard hits, and the long winter begins.

✤Pa becomes Justice of the Peace in De Smet.

✤*Five Little Peppers and How They Grew* by Margaret Sidney is published.

✤Helen Keller is born.

1881

✤Mary, Carrie, and Laura have their first photograph taken.

✤Ma and Pa take Mary to the Iowa School for the Blind in Vinton, Iowa.

✤Eliza Jane Wilder begins teaching at the De Smet school.

✤President James A. Garfield is assassinated by Charles Guiteau.

✤Billy the Kid is killed by Pat Garrett at Fort Sumner, New Mexico.

✤Clara Barton founds the American National Red Cross.

1882

✤Laura receives her teacher's certificate and begins teaching at the Bouchie School (called Brewster School in *These Happy Golden Years*).

1883

✤William Frederick "Buffalo Bill" Cody organizes the first Wild West show.

✤Standard time is established. The railroads demarcate the four time zones.

1884

✤Laura and Almanzo become engaged.

✤Almanzo and Royal leave De Smet for the New Orleans Exposition.

✤Oil is discovered in Independence, Kansas; eventually there will be twenty-three oil wells on the land that once surrounded the little house on the prairie.

✤Mark Twain's *Huckleberry Finn* is published.

✤The first sky-scraper, the ten-story Home Insurance Building in Chicago, opens.

1885

✤Laura and Almanzo are married on August 25 in De Smet.

✤David Swanzey, Carrie's future husband, suggests the name Mount Rushmore for the now-famous mountain in the Black Hills.

✤The Washington Monument is dedicated in Washington, D.C.

1886

✤Rose Wilder is born on December 5 in De Smet, Dakota Territory.

✤The Statue of Liberty is unveiled in New York harbor.

✤Coca-Cola appears on the market in Atlanta, Georgia, and is advertised as a remedy for fatigue.

1887

✤Pa and Ma, Mary, Carrie, and Grace move into their new house in town.

1888

✤Laura and Almanzo are striken with diphtheria.

1889

✤Laura and Almanzo's son is born and dies twelve days later.

✤Laura and Almanzo's house is destroyed by fire.

✤Mary graduates from the School for the Blind.

✤South Dakota becomes a state.

1890

❖Laura is twenty-three years old.

❖The Wilders leave De Smet, South Dakota, and spend a year with Almanzo's parents in Spring Valley, Minnesota.

1891

❖The Wilders move to Westville, Florida.

1892

❖The Wilders return to De Smet, South Dakota.

❖The United States government purchases the Cherokee Strip from the Cherokee Nation. The 6 million acres of land between Kansas and Oklahoma are made available to white settlers.

1894

❖The Wilders leave De Smet and travel to Mansfield, Missouri, where they purchase Rocky Ridge Farm.

1896

❖The Wilders begin construction on the first phase of their new farmhouse at Rocky Ridge—the kitchen, a front room, and an attic bedroom.

❖X rays are used for the first time in the United States for the treatment of cancer.

❖In *Plessy v. Ferguson*, the Supreme Court rules that designating "separate but equal" facilities for African Americans does not violate the 14th Amendment.

❖The Seventh Cavalry of the U.S. Army defeats Chief Sitting Bull and the Sioux Indians at the Battle of Wounded Knee. Sitting Bull dies.

❖Peanut butter is first introduced in St. Louis, Missouri.

❖Pa sells the claim and adds a two-story wing onto the house in town.

❖Helen Moore Sewell, the first illustrator of the Little House books, is born.

1897

❖John Philip Sousa writes "Stars and Stripes Forever."

1898

❖The Wilders rent out the farm and move into town. Almanzo's parents visit on their way to their new home in Louisiana.

❖The U.S. battle-ship *Maine* is blown up in the harbor of Havana, Cuba, killing more than 260 people. The Spanish-American War officially begins.

1899

❖James Wilder, Almanzo's father, dies in Louisiana.

The 1900's

1900

✤Laura is thirty-three years old.

✤The cake walk becomes the most fashionable dance in the United States.

✤Dr. Walter Reed of the U.S. Army Medical Corps discovers that the yellow fever virus ("fever 'n' ague") is transmitted by mosquitoes.

✤*The Wonderful Wizard of Oz* by L. Frank Baum is published.

1901

✤Grace Ingalls marries Nathan William Dow in De Smet on October 16. They live in Manchester, South Dakota, seven miles west of De Smet.

✤President McKinley is assassinated by Leon Czolgosz.

1902

✤Laura returns to De Smet to see Pa, who is critically ill from heart failure.

✤Charles Ingalls dies on June 8.

1903

✤Rose goes to Louisiana with Almanzo's sister Eliza Jane.

✤Orville and Wilbur Wright successfully fly a powered airplane in Kitty Hawk, North Carolina.

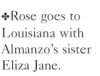

✤The teddy bear, named after President Theodore Roosevelt, is first introduced.

✤*Rebecca of Sunnybrook Farm* by Kate Douglas Wiggin is published.

1904

✤Rose is graduated from high school in Crowley, Louisiana, and takes a job as a telegraph operator in Kansas City, Missouri.

1905

✤Angeline Wilder, Almanzo's mother, dies in Crowley, Louisiana.

✤Albert Einstein formulates the theory of relativity with the equation $E = mc^2$.

1908

✤Henry Ford manufactures the first Model T automobile.

✤*Anne of Green Gables* by Lucy Maud Montgomery is published.

1909

✤Rose Wilder, age twenty-three, marries Gillette Lane in San Francisco.

✤The Lincoln-head penny is issued by the Philadelphia Mint on the 100th anniversary of Abraham Lincoln's birth. It replaces the Indian-head penny.

✤The National Association for the Advancement of Colored People is founded under the leadership of W.E.B. Du Bois.

1910

❖Laura is forty-three years old.

❖Halley's Comet is observed.

❖The Boy Scouts of America is formed.

❖The Camp Fire Girls is formed.

1911

❖Laura Ingalls Wilder publishes her first article in *The Missouri Ruralist*, titled "Favors the Small Farm Home."

1912

❖Carrie Ingalls marries David N. Swanzey on August 1.

❖The *Titanic*, an "unsinkable" luxury liner making its maiden voyage from England to the United States, collides with an iceberg and sinks, killing 1,513 people.

❖The Girl Guides, forerunner of the Girl Scouts, is formed.

❖Garth Williams, illustrator of the Little House books, is born.

1913

❖The Wilders add the parlor, library, porches, and upstairs rooms to the farmhouse at Rocky Ridge.

1915

❖Laura visits Rose, who is a newspaper reporter, in San Francisco.

1916

❖Norman Rockwell illustrates his first cover for *The Saturday Evening Post*.

1917

❖Laura helps organize the Mansfield Farm Loan Association and serves as its secretary-treasurer.

❖The United States enters World War I.

1918

❖Rose Wilder Lane and Gillette Lane divorce.

❖World War I ends.

1919

❖Congress passes the 18th Amendment, outlawing transportation and sale of alcoholic beverages and ushering in the era of Prohibition.

1920

❖Laura is fifty-three years old.

❖Hugh Lofting's *The Story of Dr. Doolittle* is published.

❖Congress passes the 19th Amendment guaranteeing women suffrage.

EQUAL SUFFRAGE LEAGUE

1922

❖Rose receives the second-place O. Henry Award for her short story "Innocence."

1924

❖Rose gives Laura and Almanzo a new car and teaches Almanzo how to drive.

❖Caroline Quiner Ingalls dies in De Smet on April 20, at age 84.

1925

❖The Scopes "monkey trial" is held in Dayton, Tennessee. John T. Scopes was arrested on May 5 for teaching the theory of evolution to his students in violation of state law. Scopes was convicted and fined $100.

❖F. Scott Fitzgerald publishes *The Great Gatsby*.

1926

❖*Don Juan*, the first talking picture presented to an audience, is shown in New York City.

1927

❖Charles A. Lindbergh, Jr., flies nonstop from New York to Paris.

1928

❖While visiting Carrie in Keystone, South Dakota, Mary suffers a stroke and dies on October 17.

❖Rose builds a rock house for Laura and Almanzo on the Rocky Ridge property.

❖Laura and Almanzo move into the rock house, and Rose moves into the farmhouse.

Spirit of St. Louis

1929

❖On Black Tuesday (October 29), over 16 million shares are dumped for whatever they could bring, causing the stock market to crash and ushering in the Great Depression.

❖Academy Awards are presented for the first time to honor outstanding achievement in filmmaking.

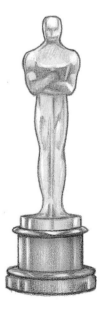

The 1930's

1930
❖Laura is sixty-three years old.

1931
❖Laura and Almanzo drive to De Smet and then to the Black Hills of South Dakota to visit Grace and Carrie.

❖The Empire State Building is completed.

1932
❖*Little House in the Big Woods*, illustrated by Helen Sewell, is published by Harper Brothers.

❖Rose Wilder Lane's *Let the Hurricane Roar* is published in serial form in *The Saturday Evening Post*.

❖Amelia Earhart is the first woman to fly solo across the Atlantic nonstop.

1933
❖*Farmer Boy* is published.

❖In an emergency session that lasts one hundred days, Congress passes legislation to aid farmers and the unemployed.

1935
❖*Little House on the Prairie* is published.

❖Rose Wilder Lane's *Old Home Town* is published.

❖Laura and Almanzo celebrate their fiftieth wedding anniversary.

❖The Homestead Act is repealed.

1936
❖Margaret Mitchell's *Gone with the Wind* is published.

1937
❖*On the Banks of Plum Creek* is published.

❖Laura and Almanzo move back into the farmhouse at Rocky Ridge after living nine years in the rock house.

❖Laura and Almanzo travel to Detroit, where Laura speaks at a book fair.

1938
❖Rose Wilder Lane's *Free Land* is published.

❖Laura and Almanzo travel with their friends Silas and Neta Seal to the west coast.

1939
❖*By the Shores of Silver Lake* is published.

❖Laura and Almanzo travel to De Smet to the Old Settlers' Day celebration.

❖John Steinbeck's *The Grapes of Wrath* is published.

The 1940's and the 1950's

1940

❖Laura is seventy-three years old.

❖*The Long Winter* is published.

❖Walt Disney's *Fantasia* opens in movie theaters.

1941

❖*Little Town on the Prairie* is published.

❖Grace dies on November 10.

❖Japanese troops attack Pearl Harbor, Hawaii. Congress declares war against Japan. Germany and Italy declare war against the United States.

❖The Mount Rushmore National Monument in South Dakota is completed after fourteen years.

1943

❖*These Happy Golden Years* is published.

1944

❖Franklin D. Roosevelt is reelected for a fourth time. He is the only president elected to four terms.

1945

❖Germany surrenders unconditionally to the Allies, ending the European phase of World War II.

❖The United States drops the first atomic bomb ever to be used in war on Hiroshima, Japan. Three days later, it drops the second atomic bomb on Nagasaki, Japan.

❖Japan surrenders and the Pacific phase of World War II ends.

❖The United Nations is formed in San Francisco.

E. B. White's *Stuart Little*, illustrated by Garth Williams, is published.

1946

❖Carrie dies on June 2.

1947

❖Garth Williams visits the Wilders at Rocky Ridge in preparation for his new illustrations for the Little House series.

1949

❖Almanzo dies on October 23, at age 92.

❖The Detroit Public Library names a branch after Laura Ingalls Wilder.

❖Arthur Miller's *Death of a Salesman* is staged on Broadway and wins the Pulitzer Prize.

1950

❖Laura is eighty-three years old.

❖The Laura Ingalls Wilder Room at the Pomona Public Library in Pomona, California, is dedicated.

❖War with Korea declared.

1951

❖The Laura Ingalls Wilder Library in Mansfield, Missouri, is dedicated.

1952

❖E. B. White's *Charlotte's Web*, illustrated by Garth Williams, is published.

1953

❖The eight Little House books are reissued with Garth Williams's illustrations.

❖War with Korea ends.

❖Puerto Rico becomes the first United States commonwealth.

1954

❖The Laura Ingalls Wilder Award is created by the American Library Association.

❖Dr. Jonas Edward Salk announces development of the first polio vaccine.

❖In *Brown v. the Board of Education*, the U.S. Supreme Court declares racial segregation in the schools to be unconstitutional.

1955

❖Jim Henson creates Kermit the Frog, the first Muppet.

1957

❖Laura dies on February 10, at age 90.

❖ Helen Moore Sewell dies.

❖Dr. Seuss's *The Cat in the Hat* and *The Grinch Who Stole Christmas* are published.

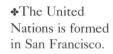

CHAPTER
Thirteen

Seeing the Little House Sites Today

TODAY YOU CAN visit many of the places Laura lived. Not all the original houses remain, but the sites are still much as Laura described them in the Little House books. Below is a list of the sites you can visit, and addresses you can use to write for more information. *Always enclose a stamp with your inquiry.*

LITTLE HOUSE IN THE BIG WOODS

The site of the cabin Laura describes in *Little House in the Big Woods* is about seven miles north of the little town of Pepin, Wisconsin. A log cabin was built recently following Laura's description of the cabin. A small museum in nearby Pepin holds memorabilia of Laura and her family and of Anna Barry, Laura and Mary's first teacher. Lake Pepin, on whose shores Laura and her family picnicked, is three blocks away from the museum.

For more information about the site and the town, and to receive a Laura Ingalls Wilder newsletter, write to:

The Laura Ingalls Wilder Memorial Society, Inc.
P.O. Box 269
Pepin, Wisconsin 54759

LITTLE HOUSE ON THE PRAIRIE

About twelve miles southwest of Independence, Kansas, on U.S. Highway 75, is the site of the Little House on the Prairie. In 1977, a one-room log cabin was built near the

site, following Laura's description of the cabin in her book. The actual well that Pa dug in 1869 is on the site.

For more information, write to:
Little House on the Prairie, Inc.
P.O. Box 110
Independence, Kansas 67301

ON THE BANKS OF PLUM CREEK

About two miles north of Walnut Grove, Minnesota, you will find the site of the Ingallses' house on Plum Creek. Nearby is the site of the dugout in which Laura and her family lived for several months. In the town of Walnut Grove, there is an Information Center and Museum with Ingalls memorabilia and other pioneer artifacts.

For information about the sites, write to or call:
The Laura Ingalls Wilder Museum
330 Eighth Street
P.O. Box 58J
Walnut Grove, Minnesota 56180
(507) 859-2358

For information about Walnut Grove's annual Laura Ingalls Wilder Pageant, write to or call:
The Wilder Pageant Committee
P.O. Box 313
Walnut Grove, Minnesota 56180
(507) 859-2174

BURR OAK, IOWA

Although Laura did not write a Little House book about the family's years in Burr Oak, Iowa, she and her family lived in this town from 1876 to 1877. Ma and Pa helped run the Burr Oak House. The hotel has been restored and is open to visitors.

For more information, write to:
Laura Ingalls Wilder Park and Museum
P.O. Box 354
Burr Oak, Iowa 52131

BY THE SHORES OF SILVER LAKE
THE LONG WINTER
LITTLE TOWN ON THE PRAIRIE
THESE HAPPY GOLDEN YEARS
THE FIRST FOUR YEARS

After the Ingallses left Walnut Grove in 1879, they settled in De Smet, Dakota Territory. They lived first in a shanty in the railroad camp on Silver Lake, then spent their first winter in the Surveyors' House close by. This house is open to visitors today, although it has been moved a few blocks north of its original location. Also in De Smet is the house Ma, Pa, and Mary lived in after Laura got married. It is now a museum containing many of the Ingallses' belongings. About 2 miles north is the site of Laura and Almanzo's first house.

For more information about the Ingallses' homes in De Smet, and to receive a newsletter, write to or call:

Laura Ingalls Wilder Memorial Society

P.O. Box 344

De Smet, South Dakota 57231

(605) 854-3383

For information about De Smet's annual Laura Ingalls Wilder Pageant, call (605) 692-2108.

THE ROCKY RIDGE YEARS

Laura and Almanzo and their daughter, Rose, moved to Mansfield, Missouri, in 1894. Their farm, Rocky Ridge, is now a museum, open to visitors from April to mid-November. Visitors can take a tour of the house and can see many of the things that Laura wrote about in the Little House books, including Pa's fiddle, Mary's Nine-Patch Quilt, and the little china jewel box Laura received for Christmas in Walnut Grove.

For more information about the museum and to receive a newsletter, write to or call:

Laura Ingalls Wilder–Rose Wilder Lane Home Association
Rt. 1, Box 24
Mansfield, Missouri 65704
(417) 924-3626

FARMER BOY

Almanzo Wilder grew up on a farm in northern New York State, about a hundred miles north of Albany. The house has been restored recently and furnished to look the way it did when he lived there.

For more information about the museum and to receive a newsletter, write to or call:
Almanzo and Laura Ingalls Wilder Association
P.O. Box 283
Malone, New York 12953
(518) 483-1207 or (518) 483-4516

Bibliography

Although space does not permit us to list all the books, articles, and other materials we consulted in preparing The World of Little House, *the following titles may be useful to readers who wish to read more about the world of Laura Ingalls Wilder.*

Anderson, William T. *The Ingalls Family Album.* De Smet, S.D.: Laura Ingalls Wilder Memorial Society, Inc. 1985.

———. *Laura Ingalls Wilder: A Biography.* New York: HarperCollins, 1992.

———. *Laura Ingalls Wilder Country.* New York: HarperCollins, 1990.

———. *A Little House Sampler.* New York: Harper & Row, 1989.

———. *The Story of the Ingalls.* 1993. Available at the Little House museums.

———. *The Story of the Wilders.* 1983. Available at the Little House museums.

Brookings County History Book. Brookings, S.D.: Brookings County History Book Committee, 1989.

Charbo, Eileen Miles. *A Doctor Fetched by the Family Dog: Story of Dr. George A. Tann, Pioneer Black Physician.* Springfield, Mo.: Independent Publishing, 1984.

Chicago and Northwestern Railway Company. *History of the Chicago and Northwestern Railway System*, Chicago.

Eggers, Elizabeth Carpenter. *Genealogy of the Carpenter-Quiner Family*, 1977.

Evans, David Allan. *What the Tallgrass Says.* Sioux Falls, S.D.: Augustana College, The Center for Western Studies, 1982.

Hechtlinger, Adelaide. *The Seasonal Hearth. The Woman at Home in Early America.* Woodstock, N.Y.: Overlook, 1986.

The Horn Book's Laura Ingalls Wilder. William T. Anderson, ed. Boston: Horn Book Magazine, 1987.

Knudsen, Charles T. *Chicago and Northwestern Railway Steampower, 1848–1956.* Chicago: Knudsen, 1965.

Kreidberg, Marjorie. *Food on the Frontier: Minnesota Cooking from 1850 to 1900 with Selected Recipes.* St. Paul, Minn.: Minnesota Historical Society, 1975.

Kurtis, Wilma, and Anita Gold. *Prairie Recipes and Kitchen Antiques*. Chicago: Bonus Books, 1993.

Lane, Rose Wilder. *Free Land*. New York: Longmans, Green, 1938.

———. *Let the Hurricane Roar*. New York: Harper & Row, 1933.

Luecke, John C. *The Chicago and Northwestern in Minnesota*. Eagan, Minn.: Grenadier, 1990.

Marcy, Randolph B. *The Prairie Traveler: A Hand-book for Overland Expeditions*. (Originally published in 1859 by the War Department.) Old Saybrook, Conn.: Applewood, 1993.

Meyer, Adolphe E. *An Educated History of the American People*. New York: McGraw-Hill, 1967.

Miller, John E. *Laura Ingalls Wilder's Little Town*. Lawrence, Kan.: University Press of Kansas, 1994.

Riley, Glenda. *Frontierswomen: The Iowa Experience*. Ames, Iowa: Iowa State University Press, 1993.

Sherwood, Leon A. *The Spirit of Independence: Independence Centennial Official History*. Independence, Kan.: Independence Centennial, Inc. 1970.

Wigginton, Eliot, ed. *The Foxfire Books*, Volumes 1–9. Garden City, N.Y.: Anchor Books, 1972–1986.

Zochert, Donald. *Laura: The Life of Laura Ingalls Wilder*. Chicago: Henry Regnery, 1976.

Index

Numbers in *italics* indicate photographs.